Table of Contents

Chapter 5: A-Z GUIDE - Comforts of Living in an RV   63

Chapter 6: Safety Whilst Living a Full-time RVer   74

Summary   87

INTRODUCTION

Question: Why would anyone voluntarily live on the road?

Answer: Anyone with a sense of adventure.

Of course there are many other reasons why you may not wish to continue living in a bricks and mortar building, other than a sense of adventure. It may work well with your employment, travelling from job to job in your RV would be far better than having to find temporary accommodation, at every stop. Or maybe you enjoy the freedom of waking up anywhere in the country that takes your fancy. Whatever the reason, once you've read this book, maybe you will yearn to join the estimated one million Americans who "live life on the road."

Not every Recreational Vehicle (RV) owner is a full-timer. Many use their RVs, to spend a few weeks or months, away from the rat race of modern life. Often the most driving reason for this, is the sense of freedom that RV living can give you. There is something unique about this lifestyle, and in this book, we want to give you a taste of what you can expect. Living a life on the road, while it seems carefree and relaxed, still needs some planning to be successful. Giving up the security of a permanent base can be daunting, and a little overwhelming for some. In this book, we will guide you every step of the way. This should be a positive adventure, one whereby you learn more about life. We want to help you make the right decisions, that suit your own needs. We humans are all individuals with different ideals and beliefs, so we will each of us have our personal reasons as to why we want to break out from the normal way of life.

Mobile living is not for everyone. Some try it and abandon it. Others love it and never turn back to the traditional lifestyle. No one can judge it until they have tried it for themselves. To overcome some of the pitfalls you may come across, it is best to do some research. Read as much as you can on the subject. This is where we hope to help you, with your pre-planning of such a major decision in your life. We will point out some of the problems you may face on the way, and how you might then overcome them. With our help, you will soon be enjoying the freedom of the road, and becoming a veteran at being a full time RVer.

RV living does not need to be a lonely affair. You will meet a whole new community of other full-time RVers, from all walks of life. Some living life on the road on a permanent basis. Others just adventuring for a few weeks or months at a time. One thing they all have in common though, is the love of freedom that RV living gives them. You will soon love your home just as much as anyone who's paying a hefty mortgage, or a high rent, on their bricks and mortar.

In this book we will go through the various stages of RV living, to help prepare you for life on the road. We will guide you, so you can consider the different types of RV's that you might purchase for yourselves. Help you to choose the right one, for your own individual circumstances, and of course your budget.

Are you retired? Are you downsizing? If you are in one of these categories, then maybe your budget will stretch to one of the more luxurious models. Though, you can live this lifestyle on a cheaper model and on a low budget. All it takes is careful planning of funds, along with the possibility of earning a small income. We will look at the various opportunities to earning a living on the road, later in the book. If you do buy an older vehicle, perhaps you can consider learning a few tips on the mechanical aspects of your new home. That way, you can attempt to do any basic maintenance yourself, helping to stave off anything major. We will consider the pro's and con's of large and smaller RVs. When we've covered all we can think of, we'll then go on to look at some other vehicles that are suitable for a mobile lifestyle.

Later, in this book, you will find a whole section on ready made tips, 111 of them, to be precise These are condensed suggestions, that will make you think about your preparations for living life on the road. They will cover most events that you may encounter, offering solutions to many problems. We have checklists for everything, whether it be setting off, or vehicle maintenance. Then we'll go on to give specific advice and tips in more detail, about your finances.

Living this alternative lifestyle does not mean that you are not a respectable tax paying citizen. You can still work for your living, just as any city or town dweller. In this book we will discuss some ideas that have proved to be successful, for those wanting to earn while on the road. You might not have much storage for things such as stock, but you can still manage a small business selling products. There are many possibilities of earning money on the road, to help fund your new lifestyle, so we will give you food for thought.

Whether you need to work or not, we have a handy chapter on finances, helping you to make your money go further. We cover how to open and run a bank account, in your nomadic lifestyle. Paying people, such as tradesmen, and depositing money can be problematic. Let us guide you through these processes. Your new lifestyle should be easier on your wallet. You are free of mortgages, sky high rents and the ever increasing bills. This should improve your finances so that if you are in any debt, you can start to pay it off. You still have to eat and pay for gas and site fees. That's why the tips in this book will help you put money in your pocket, and keep your RV on the road.

The final chapters of the book look at the importance of comfort and safety. These are two of the most common reasons as to why some people abandon the RV lifestyle. It is important to keep a focus on the good things of this lifestyle. This should, and can be, a great adventure. The wide open and long winding roads are beckoning you to go anywhere you like. Enjoy it to its fullest. With the right planning and organization, it can be a lifestyle choice you will be glad you made.

Chapter 1: Choosing an RV is all about Size and Budget

When it comes to choosing the vehicle you are going to live in, in an ideal world it would be a spacious and luxurious one. Unfortunately, reality dictates otherwise. In most cases it will involve compromises. What you buy is dependant on a number of things, not least of all, your budget. For those who have limited funds, then one option could be to look at the pre-owned market. There, you will get more "bang for your buck". Pre-owned market prices are much less than buying brand new. There are plenty of bargains to be had, but step with caution. If you do buy a used vehicle, it is well worth doing a few necessary checks before laying out any cash. Considering the money you are going to be spending, even for a used RV, then it will be prudent to have someone check everything over. Ensure that the vehicle is in full running order, and does not suffer any damp issues. Especially if you are purchasing from a private seller, without any guarantees or warranties. If you are technically minded, then you could do this yourself. If not, then hire an expert to do it for you. Further checks should include making sure there are no outstanding liens. The last thing you need is the "repo man" turning up to tow away your new home. A history check is straight forward. All you need is the VIN number of the vehicle, and then to pay a small fee to complete the check.

What is right for you and your family, depends on whether you want:

- Luxury or basic.
- Heavy or light.
- Towing or all-in.

There are almost as many internal configurations to an RV, as there external ones. This gives you plenty of options to find the right one for your own needs. If you are going to go as a full timer, then it is useful to have a fixed bed, rather than making the seats into a bed every night. Often a fixed bed is in a corner. This means that whoever sleeps against a wall, will have to climb over the other person if they need to get out of bed. There is another type of fixed bed that is becoming ever popular, called an island bed. This rectifies the problem, as it has space at either side. Smaller RV's tend not to have fixed beds, to make the most of the limited space. In these vehicles, beds make up from the daytime seating, either the dinette or the main living area seats. If you have children, then an RV with bunk beds would be useful. These can often fold against the walls, so space is at a premium during the day. If you have pets, then you want plenty of floor space for them, so they have a place to sleep at night. As you can see, just the sleeping factor alone has many options. We have only scratched the surface of a whole array of needs.

Further important considerations when purchasing your RV:

- Are you towing a car? If so then you will need a towing bar.
- What about the kitchen area? Do you need lots of space to cook, or are you content with a simple kitchenette?

- Do you need toilet facilities in the RV? Most sites have adequate sanitary facilities, but if you are likely to do much boondocking (free camping), then a toilet will be necessary.
- How separate do you need the living area from the sleeping area? This is an important factor, and will be dependant on your budget. If you feel cramped, or that there is no privacy to be by yourself, then it may make life on the road difficult.

Now that you have some understanding of factors for consideration, read on through our guide. You will learn of the different types of RV's that are available, and what they can offer. This should give you a full understanding of your choices.

CLASS A

New $80-250,000

Fuel: petrol 8-10mpg / diesel 12mpg.

Tank capacity 70-200 gallons of fuel.

Length 26-45 feet.

These vehicles can be large, with a length that can exceed forty feet. They are not ideal for navigating through small city streets, designed with a heavy bus or truck chassis. This makes them heavier to manoeuvre. Though, the large capacity fuel tank is useful, when you are traveling in areas where gas stations are few and far between. They are not too popular in Europe where the roads are often smaller, but there are some who brave it and take them over there.

Class A RV's are usually the most luxurious and spacious of the various models available. If you go for the top of the range, it can make them expensive. Many have slide out extensions, utilized when the vehicle camps up. This makes the living space larger, from around 8 feet, to around 14 feet in width, which is almost doubling the living area. The large open spacious living areas can almost resemble a small house. Often fitted to a high standard, dependent on original cost, of course. The largest of models come with a range of separate bedrooms, which can be up to 3, and all with fixed permanent beds. The living areas often have full sized couches, and the kitchen area is often stocked with standard sized white goods. For added convenience, many have their own source of generating electricity. For this they can have gas driven generators, and solar panels.

Their larger size and powerful engines means they are suitable for towing a small car. This is ideal for exploring the area, once you have parked up your RV. Due to the size, the skill set needed to drive one of these cumbersome vehicles, is better suited to the more experienced. Not as large as a house, but as close as you are going to get for a home from home experience.

If you are considering one of these vehicles, then you can find further details by searching names of manufactures such as: Thor, Winnebago, Fleetwood, Forest River and Four Winds.

CLASS B

New $60,000-125,000

Fuel: 15-30 mpg

Tank capacity 25-35 gallons of fuel.

Length 18-25 feet.

Smallest of the 3 classes of RV's, and often referred to as camper vans. Easy to use as an everyday runaround vehicle, when not in use for camping. Much easier to manoeuvre and park. Because of their size, they are economical to run, and the initial outlay for purchase is less. Most Class B's can accommodate two persons, but some have extra bedding for more, especially children. Constructed from a normal truck chassis, with the cab remaining unchanged. It is the rear that is completely redesigned. The limited space means they do not usually have permanent beds. This would restrict your living space. Often, beds make up from the seats and dinettes, with a smaller bed above the cab. To increase the headroom, roofs that rise and fall are sometimes implemented, for camping up. The layout and furnishings are not as comprehensive, or as luxurious as the Class A models. Most furniture fittings are compact, within the limited space. Some of the fixtures have a duel purpose, such as seats that turn into beds. Class B, RVs often have a small kitchenette area, with limited utilities, such as a single burner hob, and a camping fridge. The ablutions area is usually a shared toilet and shower room, though older models may not have all these facilities.

Prices can vary. Despite their small size, from new, they can still be expensive. Once again making the pre-used vans a popular option.

Great for beginners as they average around 16-20 feet in length, making them much easier to park and manoeuver. For this reason, you should not need to tow another vehicle. Unless you prefer to leave your mobile home in its pitch, once you have camped up.

For further details on these vehicles, search manufacturers such as Phoenix, Road trek, Pleasure-way, Chinook, Great West.

CLASS C

New $60,000-140,000

Fuel: 10-15 mpg

Tank holds approx 25-60 gallons of fuel.

Length 20-40 feet.

Class C RV's are seen as combining the benefits of a Class A and Class B RV's.

Class C RV's are a combination of the benefits of Class A and Class B RV's.

These vehicles are popular with families, and they are spacious enough to live in full time. They use a larger cab from a motor manufacturer, and then a purpose built body in the rear, for the living area.

The chassis size varies, in these types of RVs. Some have single, double or even triple axles. The larger sized ones are almost on a par with some of the smaller Class A RVs. These can be cumbersome for driving and parking up. The floor plans vary, some will have fixed beds and can even have an end bedroom, separating the sleeping area from the living area. Often the shower and toilet facilities can be separate, dependent on the model. They are more spacious than a Class B, resulting in a larger sized kitchen galley, with full cooking facilities.

They can be expensive to run, but much will depend on the size you choose. There are more varied options within this class.

If you are looking for manufacturers of these models, search for names such as Thor, Winnebago, Fleetwood, Coachman.

Because of their size and power, they are ideal for towing a small car.

Other Options:

If towing a small car is not ideal for you, then you could consider buying a large car and hooking it up to tow your living quarters behind you. This is an excellent option for those who like to leave their RV parked up on site. Leaving them with transport to travel around.

FIFTH WHEEL TRAILER

New $40,000-60,000

Length 30-60 feet

The fifth wheel coupling is more stable than the general hitch up travel trailer, as it attaches to the bed of a pick-up truck. They can be quite large, causing problems when manoeuvring through city streets. They are spacious and often luxurious, making them ideal for full timers. Like the class A RV's, they often have slide-outs to increase the living space, making this type of RV almost a home from home.

One drawback is that you need a specific vehicle to tow one. This has to be a pick-up truck. If you do not already own one, the cost of one can add considerably to your start up costs, as you will be buying an RV and a towing vehicle as well. They are ideal for long distance traveling, and you will have the added benefit of having an available vehicle, once you pitch the trailer.

TRAVEL TRAILER:

New $10,000-130,000

Length 16-38 feet.

Unlike the 5th wheel trailer, you can tow this trailer with a large car, or a SUV or Mini-Van.

Travel trailers can be luxurious, or basic, depending on your budget and requirements. Because of the coupling arrangements, they can be difficult to park up in a confined camping area. Often they need a little muscle power to manoeuver into place. This makes them unsuitable if you have ill health. Though there are electrical devices, such as motor movers, that make this task much easier. This makes the trailer into a large remote controlled vehicle.

Travel Trailers are an ideal introduction into the world of RV camping. They offer a level of comfort at a reasonable price.

TOY HAULER or SURV (Sports Utility RV): Another trailer.

New $60,000-100,000

These have living areas at the front, with a large storage hold underneath and towards the back. This space allows room for the storage of a small vehicle, or a couple of motorbikes. Toy Haulers can also come in the 5th wheel shape, and often have ramps to the garage facility. Even if you do not choose the 5th wheel trailer model, you will still need a large car to haul this heavier RV.

POP UP:

One of the smallest and most basic of RV's, is a trailer that folds in on itself when traveling. When you get to the camp ground, you then begin to open up your Pandora Box. Space is limited, but once you unfold the top, it is surprisingly comfortable, with fixed beds and standing room. You can still have electrical hook up, and use specialist camping heaters and cookers. It's a bit closer to actual camping than any of the other RV's as the top of the pop-up is usually canvas, like a tent. This further extends to make a large tent reception area, using poles to support it. Unfortunately, this makes them unsuitable for poor or winter weather conditions.

This is one of the most economical routes to owning an RV, with prices at around $3-4k for a new model.

TRUCK CAMPER:

A cabin that sits in the bed of a small truck. Surprisingly spacious with small kitchenette facilities. Beds make up from dinette seats. Sometimes there is even a shower or other bathroom utility fitted in place.

Manufacturers names such as Lance, Arctic Fox and Travel Lite, amongst others, make these.

Summary:

Most engined RVs in the US, use gasoline. Though, because of increased fuel efficiency, diesel is fast becoming popular. Many of the newer vehicles are offering this as an alternative option. Usually, diesel engines have an increased MPG. Diesel pump prices tend to be higher than petrol.

Now that we have helped you with deciding upon the right vehicle for your needs, let us give you one final piece of advice. Before you invest your dollars, why not HIRE an RV first, and try out the experience. This allows you to get a feel of life on the road. It is almost certain that you will be downsizing, from living in a house or apartment. This is going to take some adjusting. If you could spend a month, hiring an RV, that might be a little similar to the one you hope to own, then you will see just how much you are going to need to downsize. Fewer clothes, less pots and pans, no shed, no yard, and less bedding and books etc. There will be plenty to think about, when it comes to decluttering your life. Fear not, there are ways of making money with your throw aways. All helping to fund your future lifestyle.

A major consideration is deciding, not only how to finance your RV, but also how to finance your trip? Also, deciding in where exactly you want to explore? Planning ahead will avoid any serious mishaps, making your journey much pleasanter.

In the following chapters of this book, we will try and prepare you for your new life. The more you know, then the road ahead will be a smoother and happier one. Starting with our useful 111 tips and advice, that are set out in this book to make life on the road an easier one. This is a whole new way of living. The more you understand it, the easier the transition will be.

Chapter 2: 111 Tips to Get you Started in our New RV Lifestyle

We would also like to share some great tips with you, to help you have make that life changing decision.

Research the type of RV that will be best for you, by using our tips in chapter 1.

Whether you've bought it or not, let's give you some more tips and advice for making your RV life that much easier.

1. BE BRAVE AND SEIZE THE MOMENT. Our first, and one of our most important tips we can give you. Don't put off your decision. Before you know it, it might be too late, especially for those in advancing years. If you are certain and have the means to do take on this new lifestyle, be brave and commit to it. The old saying, "he who hesitates is lost," is quite apt. Do not let the opportunity to live your dream, pass you by. Take it with a big smile, and hit that road. We promise, you will not regret it.

2. HIRE an RV. Sound advice for those who are uncertain. Maybe you are not completely ready yet to commit everything for your life on the road, then you could always take on a long term rental. This option is ideal for those who find the appeal of RV living strong. Those who like the idea of choosing exactly where they want to wake up every morning. BUT, still cannot quite make the commitment. If you do take the rental option, then it needs to be long term

one of at least six months, as a minimum. That gives you time to experience the highs and lows of RV living. Then you might be in a better position to decide if it is the right type of life for you.

3. AN RV DOES NOT HAVE TO BE FOR LIFE. Once you have decided on your model of RV, whether you want an all in one unit, such as a class A, or one of the Trailer types, don't feel that you have to keep to it forever. If, after a year or so, you feel the RV you purchased is not everything you'd hoped it would be, then trade it for something else. Buying the right RV may take a few attempts at it before you get it right. Do not give up if your first choice doesn't work out. Try another model.

4. UPGRADE If you are happy with your RV, and don't want to go to the expense of changing it, then just add to it. Many additions to your RV can be DIY projects, such as fitting solar panels, or creating more storage space. Sometimes little changes like these, can make your RV more homely and comfortable. All going towards making your RV lifestyle more enjoyable. Though, beware when dealing with electrics or gas work. Leave this type of upgrade to the experts, or it may be the death of you, literally.

5. DO NOT limit your search for an RV to your local area. Look nationwide and make it part of the adventure in your lifestyle change. Dependent on where you live, options for purchasing an RV in your small area, could be few. You may end up buying one that is not suitable, if you are not willing to spread out your search area. Though, should this happen, you can always trade it later, but this can come with a financial penalty. If RV dealers are few and far between in your area, then look further afield, and enjoy the journeys.

6. If you are going to buy one of the TRAILER OPTIONS as your new RV home, then you need to research whether or not your towing vehicle can take the weight. Large trailers need powerful vehicles to tow them, especially if you are visiting hilly or mountainous areas. Our tip would be to buy the biggest and most powerful vehicle that is suitable for towing an RV, that you can afford. Should you change to a larger RV trailer at a later date, then the towing vehicle will cope with it, and you won't need to buy a new car as well.

7. VISITING FAMILY AND FRIENDS IS EASIER - Modern living often means that your family members are spread out, all over the country, if not the world. What better way to visit them than in your own RV. You can visit loved ones you have not seen in a long while. You will not cause them any burden, as you have your own place to stay. One that you have brought with you. Celebrate your new lifestyle by embracing your newfound freedom and seeing family more often.

8. MAKING NEW FRIENDS - Your whole world of acquaintances is about to explode. As you move on and stop off at places, you will continue to meet new people. Some you will bump into time and again, as they travel around too. The whole RV lifestyle is a social orientated one, and you will meet likeminded folk, who you can exchange your stories with, of places you have stopped at and liked or disliked.

9. CHANGE YOUR SCENERY AS OFTEN AS YOU WISH - The full splendor of the USA, is your potential viewing, right from your own mini living room. Whether it's mountains, beach or woodlands, they are all available to you with the RV lifestyle. Imagine what this will do for your

mental spirit and well being, waking up to views that make you smile for the rest of the day.

10. BEING OUTDOORS IS HEALTHY: Whilst you won't actually sleep outside, unless you want to, it is the outdoor life that will be a great benefit. A mountain trek, or a walk through the woodlands, are all options available to you in your new active lifestyle. The beauty of it is, that you can do as much, or as little, as you want.

11. YOU GET TO CHOOSE YOUR CLIMATE: Missing the sun? Got those cold winter blues? Then take yourself off and follow the sun and the heat. Wake up to al fresco breakfast, in glorious sunshine. Or maybe ski-ing's more your thing. Just head to the mountains and get out on the slopes. That is the beauty of it all. YOU get to choose, AND, you can move around them all if you wish.

12. CHANGE YOUR NEIGHBORS: This is like no other vacation, if you don't like your destination, or your neighbors, move on and change them. When you do like everything, then you have the option to stay as long as you like. What a wonderful life-changing choice!

13. REDUCE THOSE CLEANING BLUES: This is more so if you have lived in a large house. You still need to keep your RV spic and span, because of the limited space. It will be so much easier than keeping a whole house clean and tidy. This leaves more time to enjoy life.

14. NO MORE GARDENING: Even if you do like gardening, you'll be too busy enjoying yourself with the great outdoors. The scenery through your window is your new giant garden. For many, no garden to maintain is a positive

thing, cutting down on physical labor and no more spending money on expensive plants. Again, it also leaves more time to enjoy other important aspects of life.

15. LOWER COST OF LIVING: The cost of life on the road does not compare to the cost of living in a house or apartment. Have a look at these relevant tips of advice below.

16. If you have given up your mortgage or rent, then you will now be paying site fees. Though even these can be optional, should you choose to wild camp and make the most of free camping. When you stay at an organized site, the fees are inexpensive in comparison to a bricks and mortar home.

17. Energy bills will reduce. Even if you use electric hook up. There is also the option to provide your own power via a generator or solar panels.

18. There is, of course, the initial expense of purchasing your RV, and unlike a bricks and mortar home, it will depreciate over time. The good news is, that a loan can be tax deductible.

19. There are other expenses, regardless of your lifestyle choice, such as food, clothing, cell and internet, gasoline usage, medical expenses and insurances. Though you may find that these will be less. That's the beauty of RV living, you have much more control over how much and what exactly you want to spend your money on.

20. MORE RELAXED LIFESTYLE: The freedom of the road can help lower stress levels. With RV living you will live a much more relaxed lifestyle. Especially as you reduce your financial outgoings. If you had built up debts, just knowing that you are now paying them off, is a fantastic relief. Money worries can be a thing of the past,

21. DOWNSIZING CAN BE GOOD FOR YOUR HEALTH: Selling on the family home, because your children have left to live their grown up lives elsewhere, happens to a lot of retired people. Living in an RV is a much easier lifestyle, once you have adjusted to the more confined space. It will become almost automatic, being a minimalist. The constant need to upgrade your home, will become a thing of the past.

22. ALLOCATE WHO DOES WHAT: This is in relation to living together harmoniously, in such a confined space. It is essential that each person is aware of what they are responsible for. Make a clear plan with regards to chores. It would be ideal to create a rota for who gets to do certain jobs, such as fill the water tank, cleaning, cooking, even going to the launderette. Life will be so much smoother when everyone knows what they are doing. This ensures all the chores get done and you are comfortable and clean in your smaller home.

23. SHOPPING: Due to lack of storage, you are best to limit the amount of shopping you do, to a few days at a time. That way you can keep things fresh as well. Plus, you don't want too much weight in tins and liquids, especially when you're on the move. It is not a good idea to store too much food.

24. THE RIGHT RV WILL MAKE A BIG DIFFERENCE: The most important tip we can give you, and this has to be no.1 on your list. Choose the right vehicle and you will enjoy the experience. The wrong one has the potential to make life miserable, or cause more hard worry as you trade it in for a different model. We have stressed that this can be done at any time, but life would be so much easier, if you have done your research and purchased the perfect RV from the   word   "go."

25. FIND A REPUTABLE DEALER: Buy from a reputable dealer, to make sure that everything is covered, should there be any mechanical or structural problems. Of course you can never be 100% certain that any vehicle is in top condition. There's nothing worse than finding out something is wrong, after the purchase. Being with an established dealer will give you a good warranty, helping to ease any worries because you know you can always take the vehicle back for any repairs.

26. BUYING A USED RV: There is nothing wrong with buying second hand, plus, this will save money. Often the mileage is low on second hand RVs, because they are not generally vehicles that are used every day. Most people just use them for holidays. You can save yourself a considerable amount of money by buying pre used, and you can always modify it to make it more personalised.

27. GET IT CHECKED BY AN EXPERT: This is if you are not buying from a dealer. Have a professional look over the RV. It will cost a fee, but it could save you money in the long run. Even for a pre used RV, it is better if you buy from a dealer, so you have a certain degree of cover for any initial teething problems that you may experience.

28. EXTENDED VEHICLE WARRANTY MAKES A BIG DIFFERENCE: Give yourself even more peace of mind by

taking out an extended warranty on your RV. This will cover you once the manufacturer's, or dealer's warranty has expired. They can be expensive, but if you have a mechanical failure, then it will soon pay for itself and you will be glad you took it out.

29. BREAKDOWN AND RECOVERY MAKE A BIG DIFFERENCE: Always better to be safe than sorry. Recovering a broken down vehicle, especially the size of an RV, is an expensive business. Always make sure that you have the best breakdown recovery you can afford, just incase. It is also handy to have that bit of extra cover for alternative accommodation. Then you have somewhere to stay, should your RV be in for repairs for any length of time. Let's not forget, this is not just a vehicle, but your home too.

30. PERSONAL EFFECTS INSURANCE IS ESSENTIAL: DO NOT assume that your RV insurance will cover your personal effects, it does not. Losing what little personal belongings you have, will not be a good experience. If you are not covered to replace them, this will only make a bad situation worse should anything happen to your contents, such as robbery or breakages.

31. DOWNSIZING IS ESSENTIAL: No matter how large your RV is, the contents of your home will not fit into it. If you are looking to go full time, then much of that stuff you own is going to have to go. Even if you are not planning to be a full timer and just going on a vacation, you have to be ruthless in what you pack into an RV. Having a clear-out can also increase your finances. The income from the sales of your personal belongings, at places such as online auction houses, or garage sales, will help to fund your new lifestyle.

32. CHECKLIST FOR IMPORTANT DOCUMENTS: Make a list of the essential documents that you are going to need, such as Driving license, Passport, Vehicle documents, Emergency telephone contact details, medical details, and any more that you can think of. Oh, and don't forget the Bank cards. Check your list on a regular basis, whilst on the road. Then you can update it when necessary.

33. CHECKLIST FOR PERSONAL BELONGINGS: To ensure that you have packed all the contents that you are going to need, write a list, over time. There is nothing worse then being 100 miles into your journey, and realizing that you forgot to pack the pillows! To make this task easier, try doing it in alphabetical order:

A = Awning and fittings, Aluminum foil.

B - Books, Brushes (hair), Brush and dust pan, Bedding, Batteries, Bug sprays, Belts, Bags - freezer, bin, sandwich, handbags, Barbecue equipment, Boots.

Take your time over the creation of this list, don't just rush it in an hour. If you are to get it right, it should take weeks to plan.

34. CHECKLIST OF VEHICLE FOR MOVING ON - Get yourself a routine of checking the safety of the vehicle, every time you are ready to move on from camping. You'll soon get the hang of it, and find that performing these tasks becomes automatic. Though it might be a good idea to have a tick off checklist, so you don't forget anything. Every task is crucial for safety reasons. REMEMBER, you are in a large moving vehicle so you don't want to be doing

anything silly, like leaving outer locker doors open or skylight windows open. All such possibilities are easily eliminated if you have a simple check list before you move on.

35. **PURGE THE TANKS**: Ensure you have emptied all your waste water tanks, and your clean water supply tank. Don't forget the cassette toilet too. Carrying an unnecessary heavy load of water will have a negative impact on fuel economy, and you don't want the risk of any nasty smells either.

36. **FASTEN DOWN THE HATCHES** - Fasten down all windows, doors and drawers, so they will not come flying open while on the move. The last thing you want while driving down the freeway, is your contents flying all over the place. Hopefully, these tasks will be covered in your "moving on," to do list.

37. **SWITCHING OFF THE FRIDGE**: If it is a two way refrigerator, 115v or 12v dc, then you can switch to the RV battery while traveling. REMEMBER to turn it off when you stop, or it will drain your RV battery.

38. DO NOT pack heavy items in the overhead cabinets. The weight could force cupboard doors open, spilling out the contents of that cupboard that you remembered to baton down so well. For good balance you want to keep heavy items low down when in storage, especially when moving.

39. CLEAR ALL SURFACES of loose items when you are on the move. it is so to forget this one, until you hear things clanging around as you are driving along.

40. LOVE YOUR RV - Learn everything you can about your new living space. Understand what it needs to make it function as your home. Keep everything in tip top condition, from general cleaning duties to the maintenance related work. The more you understand your new home, the more you can do to sort out any little problems you may encounter. Not only will this help in maintaining your RV's value, but you will be much more comfortable and content.

41. MAINTENANCE CHECKLIST: Another regular chore deserving of an all important checklist. The following are to ensure all is in good working order before you set off:

42. CHECK FLUID LEVELS: Your vehicle is your home, so take good care of it. Check these levels in a regular basis: oil, brake fluid, windshield washer, engine coolant water, power steering.

43. ODORLESS RV - Help keep your RV smelling fresh and clean by keeping the grey water and black water storage tanks clean. They need emptying at regular intervals. Though that is not enough stop any bad smells. Give them an occasional flush out by using the built in pressure valve. Then rinse them with an approved cleaner. When you do this, ensure that you leave a little water in. It will break down that chemical that breaks down the waste.

44. CHECK BATTERY CONNECTIONS: This includes any leisure battery too. Make sure they are fully charged. Then check that all connections are functional and attached.

45. CHECK LIGHTS: Ensure brake lights are working, especially if you are towing. Check all lights that should flash and flicker to make sure they are still doing so. Check reverse lights are still working.

46. CHECK YOUR HORN IS IN WORKING ORDER: Especially as you are driving a large vehicle.

47. CHECK THE BRAKES: This goes without saying, but you must do this on a regular basis.

48. CHECK TIRE PRESSURE: Ensure you are aware of what pressure each tire should be.

49. CHECK AXLE LOAD: If you are too heavy for your axle, it will cost you more in fuel, and could make your RV unstable. Learn how to check the overall weight, it will be worth it.

50. LEARN HOW TO DISTRIBUTE YOUR LOAD: Again, it is worth learning the weak points of your vehicle, where you should place heavy loads. This makes economical sense for your vehicle.

51. STAND OUT IN THE DARK - Often it can be quite late at night when you return to your RV, making it a little tricky to find it in the dark, if you have been out without it. A great tip is to add reflective tape or light reflectors to the steps and sides of your walkways. This makes life so much easier to finding your way back home in the dark.

PRE-PLAN EVERYTHING

52. PLAN YOUR ROUTE: Have a good idea where you are going, even if you change your mind once you are on the road. Plus, you may want to let friends and family have an idea where you are in the world.

53. HAVE A SITE BOOK: It doesn't hurt to have a book of official camping sites situated along your route. Don't just rely on the internet as you may not always have access. There are over 16,000 official campgrounds in the US alone. Around half of these are in national parks and forests. Many located in, and on the outskirts, of big cities. Meaning you can still enjoy city life as well.

54. SLOW DOWN your pace - A big mistake many new full-timers commit, is the urge to travel everywhere all at once. Zig-zagging across the country trying to take in as much as possible, or rushing around trying to visit family members. Stop! Slow Down! Enjoy where you are. Move

on when you're ready. There's no need to rush. Those amazing scenic places will still be there next week.

55. JOIN A CLUB: There are many clubs you can join. Some specific to RVers, others just related to camping. Most of the clubs offer large discounts at their sites, if you are a member. Membership is not expensive and is quickly recovered in site fees you have saved.

56. LEARN ABOUT THE CULTURES YOU ARE VISITING: This is relevant to those adventurous enough to go touring the world. You don't have to speak the lingo, but it is only courteous to behave by the local laws. It's worth doing a bit of homework on the places you are going to visit. This will ensure that you get full enjoyment and understand what you can expect when you get there.

57. BUDGET BUDGET BUDGET: Especially if you are new to traveling. Sit down and estimate how much you are going to need for your trip. Include all the essentials, as well as a few luxuries. Ideally, you also need a contingency fund for emergencies..

58. MEDICAL COVER: Understand how the hospital systems work of the places you are visiting, you never know if you are going to need it. This is more so if you are traveling to another country. Not every country has the same system as your own. Sites often have local contact numbers in their reception areas, for doctors, chemists, police, e.t.c.

59. STORAGE SPACE: If you have downsized your brick and mortar home already, then you will be glad you did it. No matter how large your RV is, you will still have limited storage. Gone are the days when you had around 10 pans in your kitchen, now you should just 3 at the most. Much the same goes for everything. Fewer belongings is better. Make use of small boxes with lids to keep things tidy, especially when on the move. Plus, you will know where everything is. Organizing doesn't have to rule your life.

Once you've done the initial storing of things, it will just become habit to put them back in their place.

60. **MEALS:** Cooking will be much the same as it was before you set off. It helps if you always have a meal in, just incase you get stuck somewhere and cannot get access to shops. Storage may limit how many meals you can plan, but a few emergency tins and packets are a must.

PERSONAL FINANCES

61. GETTING A LOAN: Could be an option if you are going to continue to work. Don't make those monthly payments too high though, you might struggle and add to your financial burden. It does mean you could have the perfect RV for your needs. (see chapter 3).

62. SELL YOUR HOME: If you're looking to go full time. The money from the sale is an ideal way to fund your new life. If you're a retired family person, then perhaps the children have left home and you are downsizing anyway. Buying a smaller home may leave some money left over to invest in a life on the road, for a while.

63. RENT OUT YOUR HOME: Another way that your home can help finance your new life. If you're not sure about living full time in your RV, then you could rent out your home, instead of selling it. This will ensure the mortgage or rent payments are being upheld, while you are on the road. If you have paid your mortgage in full, then it's a welcome regular income. Of course it does mean accommodating strangers in your home. Also, you can rent it via an agency, for a fee, leaving all the hard work up to them.

64. **WIFI** - Getting online is an absolute necessity for many RVers. The advent of the mobile phone, and its ability to connect to the internet, has revolutionised mobile

browsing. Though data can be expensive. To reduce data costs, you should make use of the wifi available on most camp grounds. It's often free, or there's a small fee. There can be a problem of a poor signal, especially if you are on a large camp ground. For around $20, you can fit a wifi extender into your RV, which will increase the signal from the base station.

65. WORK ON THE MOVE: This is a great way to continue financing your trip of a life time. Especially if you are a full timer. Even if retired. You will need to keep a record of all your income for when you fill out the appropriate tax forms for your country. There is no reason that you cannot be self employed whilst moving around. Here's a few brief suggestions on how to earn an income, while living on the road:

66. FIND LOCAL TEMPORARY WORK: Such as on farms, picking fruit and vegetables. It is hard work, and you do need to be quite fit do this.

67. CAMP SITE WORK: Many campsites will hire RVrs to do general maintenance duties around the site, maybe man the shop or reception.It could be a great way to fund your new life.

68. ARTISAN ITEMS: This is ideal for those who have a craft, such as jewelry making, woodwork, making greetings cards, knitting. You can sell online, or even travel around the relevant craft fairs to sell your wares. You would also need to consider storage for your stock.

69. WORK ONLINE: This is a great way of earning an income. Many sites have internet access, sometimes for a small fee. You could also use cell phones and tablets for internet access. Many public areas now give free internet access, particularly cafes, bars and restaurants. Here are some more tips on internet work:

70. **ONLINE AUCTION SITES**: Though storage space for stock may be an issue for you, but you can post your sales from and to, anywhere in the world.
71. FREELANCE WRITING: There are many websites where you can find work writing, and get paid via Paypal, or into your bank account.
72. WRITE A TRAVEL BLOG: While not an immediate money spinner, running a travel blog of your trip may bring in some great followers. The more popular the blog, then you can earn an income by selling advertising space on your pages.
73. DROP SHIPPING: All you need is an organized mind and access to the internet. Drop shipping means the goods go straight from the supplier, and you don't need storage space. Do your homework and find reliable drop shipping suppliers who won't let you down, by not having the stock in that your customer has ordered. With time and experience this can be a lucrative business, whilst on the road.

74. **DOMICILE**: When you are on the move, it is useful if have a place you can call your base, even if just for your tax returns etc. Many choose a relative's address, or the state they last resided in. There can be advantages in choosing a different one. States such as Texas and Florida have no sales tax, so that can be handy. Taxes such as health insurance, vehicle insurance and other everyday taxes, can vary from state to state. This means it is worthwhile doing your homework before you make your decision where to register your domicile.

75. DEBT: You may already be having financial difficulties before you begin this life. If so, then the lower cost of living should mean that you can come to arrangements to pay monthly amounts to your existing debts. Particularly so, if you continue to work. Do not let having debt put you off choosing this lifestyle. Often that may be the main reason people have chosen simplicity, to escape the cumbersome

cost of living. Debt can still be manageable.

LUXURIES YOU CAN TAKE WITH YOU

76. COMFORTABLE BED: You can still have a good night's sleep in a comfortable bed, especially if you purchase an RV with fixed beds. Even the seats or dinettes that make up into beds, are usually quite comfortable, with thick cushioning. You can still use your sheets, duvets and pillows, so you feel cosy as warm toast.

77. HOT RUNNING WATER: Most RVs have a boiler to heat up water.

78. SHOWER. Larger RVs have a shower with hot running water.

79. TOILET FACILITIES: Often this may be in the shower room. You will need to learn how to fill and empty the cartridges or fixed tanks, which are usually done at chemical disposal points on the larger sites. Plus filling up the flush area. To break down the waste you will need to put chemicals in the tank, but a sweet smelling liquid can go in the flush.

80. TELEVISION: This set up can be as complex or simple as you chose. It is also dependent on the country you are visiting, and what is available. You could learn how to stream your TV programs and films through a lap top or tablet.

81. COLD FOOD: The larger your RV the better your kitchen facilities will be. A fridge is top of the list on most kitchenettes, some even have freezer compartments.

82. COOKED MEALS. Stoves and hobs are fitted into kitchenette galleries. Again, the larger your RV, the better the cooking facilities.

83. LIGHTING: Even if you're not hooked up to the mains, you can run your lighting on the leisure battery.

84. LED LIGHTING: If your RV doesn't already have these, then it is highly recommended that you replace your bulbs with these. They are far more economical to run, and you will see the benefits almost instantly.

85. HEATING: Usually runs on the propane gas system, unless you have a blower system inbuilt in your RV. If you do opt for an electrical heater, purchase one with a low wattage. Many sites only allow a limited amount of electrical power to each hook up.

86. MICROWAVES and SLOW COOKERS: are ideal means of cooking in an RV. You must have low wattage models, so you do not overload the site supply.

87. CLOTHING: As always, much depends on your storage space on how much clothing you can keep. You can still iron your clothes, but you will need to stop at launderettes to do washing. Most of larger camp ground will have them on site. You can even hang laundry out in the sun on a make shift line, to save on drying costs. Though laundry usually have tumble dyers as well.

88. PETS: Most sites allow well behaved pets. If you are traveling overseas with pets, you will need to find out the local laws on bringing pets into their country. Usually a pet needs to go into quarantine for a few weeks, so allow for this if traveling overseas.

89. HOTEL BOOKINGS: There is no reason why you can't enjoy the odd night in a hotel room, or at relatives, and live in bricks and mortar for a few nights. Be flexible, that's the whole point of living on the road. Nothing is set in stone.

90. STAYING PUT FOR A WHILE: You don't have to travel all the time. Take your time when you find somewhere you like. It's not just about traveling, it's about loving your life. If you're retired you may be looking for a warm climate, and then staying there for months. Nothing wrong with that. You choose.

NEED   TO   KNOW

91. PROPANE GAS: used for - refrigerators, heaters, water heaters, stoves.

92. SAFETY FIRST: Ensure the gas system is turned off when you travel.

93. AIR CONDITIONING: Some RV's come with ready installed units, and are a real boon when the temperature rises. If yours has no Air Con, then you can buy portable units for your RV.

94. DUAL BATTERY SYSTEMs: This includes the engine battery, and a leisure appliance battery. Both batteries charged via the engine's alternator, when on the move. The leisure battery can also charge through the connection to the camp ground's mains power.

95. POWERING APPLIANCES: Appliances in an RV, such as cooler, water pump, lighting, and even some TV's, usually run on duel power, working off mains electric 110v, or the battery 12v. Though, using many appliances will soon drain the leisure battery. When on full charge, this will last on average around 12 hours. When you connect to the mains power at the camping ground, most appliances will switch over to run off 110v, rather than run off the 12v battery.

96. AIR VENTS: Check the air vents for obstructions, on a regular basis. Debris can blow into them, when you're on the move. Keep all filters clean, or if damaged, then

replace them. Vents should always be clear, especially internal ones, such as inside the cooler.

97. CONDENSING UNIT: Check this is clean and that there are no obstructions, so the air flow is fresh.

98. VOLTAGE of most RV's run between 110-130 volts, but averages 120 volts.

99. CARTRIDGE TOILET OR TANK: It is important to empty this on a regular basis, and keep it clean. The base of the unit holds the waste, and chemicals you pour into there, break it down. The upper tank holds the water for flushing the toilet. This is where you can put the nicer smelling liquids. If you have a Black water tank, instead of a cartridge toilet, then check out our tips for keeping it clean.

100. PARKING: The larger your RV, the more problematic parking will be. Check that your camp ground accepts RVs, especially if you are longer than 30ft. If your RV hasn't already got a reversing camera fitted, then consider getting one. They are a great help, once you get used to using them.

101. WILD CAMPING: Also known as boondocking. Many prefer the security of an organized camp ground to stay in. If you are adventurous enough, there are some great places to stop that are completely free of charge. Be aware, you cannot camp where ever you like, and especially not on private land, or you may find yourself having free B&B in the local jail! There are many guides and books on this subject. They will point you to the safest and legal places to wild camp. As you become a seasoned camper, you will learn the best places.

102. OFF SITE: Sometimes the sun may be setting, and the nearest official camping ground is still many miles away. Caught out like this, then you could consider Truck Stops, Outlet Malls or Wal-Mart parking lots. Some roadside hotels often have hook up points (for a small fee). Though

do not just assume you can park anywhere without permission. Always try to check with the local manager before you camp up.

103.   SITE FEES: are going to vary, particularly if you are traveling overseas. That is why it is a good idea to plan ahead. Once you are more experienced of living on the road, you may become braver and just turn up without a booking. Prices for full hook up usually range between $10-$50 per night. As mentioned in a previous tip, join one of the many camping clubs, and get discounts on your site fees.

104.   MAIL DELIVERY: You can arrange to have mail delivered to local post offices en route. It is also known as the Post Restante service in many countries, which is the same as the General Delivery Service in the USA. Using this service incurs a small fee, but is useful if you are expecting important mail. They often keep your post for up to 30 days, but do check out individual services.

105.   CASH: Staying in your own country should not raise any issues with this one. If you travel overseas though, you will need to find out the local currency. Try and get to grips with the conversion rates. Using your bank card should not be a problem. Travellers cheques are also good, if you lose them, no one else can cash them, and you can get them replaced. This is another "do your research," because everyone does it differently. Carrying a lot of cash is not recommended. Even having a hide-safe in your vehicle is not too wise. Much of Europe uses Euros, making travel easier. There are still many countries that keep their own currency, such as the UK, so be aware before you get there.

106.   DRIVING: If you only have a single driver, this may be problematic if they become ill. It might be a good idea to have a back up plan, such as a relative on stand by, should something happen. This is not an easy one to organize. It's better if everyone you are travelling with has

to learned to drive the RV. Even if only for emergency situations.

107. **INSURANCES:** This is only a brief reminder to make sure you think about it. Know and understand exactly what you need to set in place, before you set off. For instance, it is unlikely that your motor insurance covers all your personal belongings. Find out from your insurance provider, don't just assume. Health insurance needs checking out as you are on the move, so normal coverage may not be enough. It is country dependent. It is most definitely worth checking that you have insurance cover for everything. It is more expense, but one of those necessary ones.

108. CONTACT WITH THE OUTSIDE WORLD: There is no reason why you should not have a cell phone. In fact, it is one of the gadgets that you should keep. From this you can access the internet, use it to stream media to your TV, and keep in contact with family and friends. Today's technology means that you can keep in touch almost everywhere, just with the press of a few buttons. Don't cut yourself off from the world, there really is no need.

109. RELAX: Because that's what RV living is meant to be all about. Enjoy your surroundings by taking in the scenery. Enjoy meeting new people. Even if you need to work to fund your lifestyle, you can still enjoy the freedom that living on the road brings with it.

110. MAKE FRIENDS - lots of them, because they will be a great source of information, tips and tricks. Your fellow RVers may have been doing this for years, and are well versed in what does and doesn't work. Not only can you increase your social circle, but you can also tap into their experience.

111. FINALLY - No amount of tips and tricks can cover everything. The longer you travel on the road, the more you will realise what is important to you as an individual.

Make a list as you travel, of all the things you feel you need. Things that felt important in your previous home, no longer matter in this new and simpler lifestyle. Living in an RV can help you step aside from the rampant commercialism, that is the mainstream of modern living. You are now living a life closer to nature, so get out and enjoy it.

Chapter 3: How to Earn an Income, on the Road

We have touched on the options of working for a living, while on the road. Have a quick look, if you haven't already done so, at chapter 2 points 55-63, of our essential tips. In this chapter we will go into more detail of the ways you can fund your RV lifestyle. Finding suitable employment can be an important element for many RV'ers. Especially if you do not have the means to "up sticks" and travel around the country, or even the world. It is possible, and practical, to work while you travel. This can be a major source of funding that will enable you to live the RV lifestyle, both long or short term. Life on the road does not have to be as expensive as traditional living within a fixed base. Most people still need to earn a living to pay for the basics, and the odd luxury. Regardless of your personal circumstances, even if you're retired or not in the best of health, you can still earn a living whilst on the road. There are so many different options available. There is something out there that will to suit everyone.

Let's take a look at those previous tips, in bit more detail. To help you find work, there are many websites that match workers with employers, such as workamper.com.

SEASONAL EMPLOYMENT:

There are seasonal jobs, all around the world, and all year round.

Working on farms picking crops, such as fruit and vegetables. This type of work is best for those who are fit and active, as it can be quite labor intensive. It usually involves lots of bending down, dependant on the crop. It will provide a temporary income. You may even get to eat the crops that you're picking. Whilst hard work is prerequisite, it should also be satisfying as you will be working out doors. Being close to nature can give you a new lease of life, especially if most of your employment has been city based and indoors. This type of work is often found with local advertisements. It might be worth asking the camp host if they are aware of any local crop growers, looking for field workers for their harvest. There are also online job sites that include seasonal work in their listings.

Not all seasonal work is crop gathering, this is just one option for harvest time.

You could consider applying for work on the Mesa Verde, which is a national park . There are many camp grounds within this designated UNESCO World Heritage Site. These jobs are often tourism related:

Retail - sales, shelf filling, serving, cleaning.

Catering - sales, cooking, waitering, bar work, cleaning.

Sports related - activities assistant, pool staff, lifeguards, instructors, camp site workers putting tents up, creche work, horse work, bike work, golf, fishing, ski ing, water sports, cleaners.

Hotelier work - maintenance, housekeeping, room or maid services, reception, security.

Driving - mini buses, tours, taxis in local towns.

Language facilitator - Translators (if you have more than one language).

There are a vast variety of seasonal jobs, especially near the coast or mountains. It's worth pointing out that those who can work the whole season, usually April to October, are often preferred to those who want shorter term contracts.

To start your search for this type of employment, try the online website www.coolworks.com. You can apply well ahead of time and set up work in different places. This way you can still keep on the move, working in different areas as you travel. Some seasonal positions come with a parking space for your RV, often situated in the most picturesque areas of the country. If money is not so essential for you, then you could consider volunteer work. This is a great way to get to know the locals, and to be able to contribute to the communities that you are visiting.

If you are considering working overseas, don't forget to check out if you need a work visa or permit. Do your research and find out about all the legal paraphernalia that might go with such a commitment.

CAMP SITE WORK: Also known as "workamping"

This involves working for a number of hours a week, usually around 10-20, at the camp ground where you are staying. In return, you may get free camping fees, and hook up. Sometimes the employer will pay the minimum wage as well, for whichever state you are in. This type of work can vary and include jobs such as, maintenance, site hosts - greeting new arrivals, allocating pitches, taking ground rent, site shops, general cleaning, grass cutting, gardening tasks and landscaping skills. If you like meeting people and getting involved in the site that you're staying at, then this can be a great way of life. Finding this type of work is fairly straightforward. You could ask around at different sites when you arrive, and stay a while longer once you find work. If you want a more organized approach, there are many websites to search on, such as www.work-for-rvers-and-campers.com, www.snowbirdrvtrails.com and www.camphost.org. They deal with employment at camp grounds all around the US. It is possible to find seasonal work all year round, but you will need to go to the winter sport villages during the colder months. Skiing villages will be busy and wanting temporary staff. For employment in the winter months, you can try resorts in Colorado, such as Aspen, Beaver Creek and Breckenridge, to name but a few.

If you've never done anything like this before, then a quick web search will bring up various sites where RVer's, just like you, are discussing their working life. They are happy to share in their experiences and let you know of the good and bad points of working on the road. As you become more experienced with each year, you could find yourself applying for the team leaders, management and supervisory posts. From national parks, resorts, ranches and farms, to camp grounds, ski ing villages and water based entertainment, it is all there for the picking. There are an abundance of temporary jobs where you can gain experience, and have fun all at the same time.

ARTISAN ITEMS:

Turn your crafting hobbies and hand made goods, into a lucrative business. With the added bonus of being an RV owner, you can travel the country, attending craft fairs and markets to sell your wares. The beauty of this type of work, is that the possibilities are endless. Almost everyone can turn their hand to some craft or other, whether it be:

Making costume jewelry.

Hand Made Greetings cards, for all occasions, all year round. People will pay that little bit extra to have individual and unique hand made items.

Knitting or crochet. If you have either of these skills, you can offer an array of goods, such as clothing, dolls, computer sleeves, covers for digital readers or phones, the list is endless. If you've never knitted before, then give it a go. It is one of those relaxing and productive pastimes, for male and females alike. Plus, it might just earn you a living.

Woodwork. Turn your hand to making toys or furniture and gifts. If you are a skilled carpenter already, then you may find work such as maintaining premises. You might even offer your services to fix or improve furniture in your fellow RVers vehicles.

Photography or artwork - sell your prints or pop them in frames. With the explosion of digital cameras and cell phones, it seems everyone can be the next Ansel Adams or Annie Leibovitz. While visiting stunning locations you could photograph or paint the scenery, and then sell them on to tourists.

Tapestries or cross stitching can be stunning once complete, and if done well, will sell on.

Creating decorative items is an ideal activity for an RV lifestyle. The goods you make should be relatively small and light, making them easy to store. You could do your work in the dinette area, or sat out in the sunshine with a panoramic view.

Many local towns you drive through on your travels, will have marketplaces, flea markets and craft fairs. For a small fee you could arrange ahead to hire a table for the day, and sell your goods. Alternatively, you could consider selling your hand made items on the internet. Online auction houses, such as eBay, or other craft commercial websites, such as Etsy are popular with buyers of hand crafted items. You can even have a go at creating your own website, as an extra platform to sell from.

USING YOUR OWN SET SKILLS:

Utilize any other skills that you already have, such as hairdressing, DIY, gardening, mechanics or even cleaning. These are all skills that others may be happy to pay for, or even barter. You cut your fellow travellers' hair, whilst they fix your chair, so to speak. ✳ Trade Skills

Once you land at your camp ground, try putting a small ad in a local shop window to let your new neighbors know about your

Home Service Crafts
House Sitting

46

services. Take photographs of your successes, and build up a portfolio to show future customers. It's up to you to prove how trustworthy and reliable you are, because locals may be wary of travellers. A friendly and open disposition will go a long way to earning their trust.

You could also consider studying while on the move, as there are many online courses whereby you never need to attend a classroom. You could use your studies to improve your employment prospects. It's a good message for future employers. Informing them that, whilst you might live your life a little different to the norm, you still care about being competitive in the working market. Plus, studying at your leisure means that you may well enjoy it. It's not quite the same as being at school where you had to do it. You are doing it for you, and no one else.

WORKING ONLINE:

With the explosion in the ownership of smart cell phones and tablets, and with wide cell network coverage, it has never been easier to get online. Even while you are on the move. The ability to connect to the web wherever you are, means that online working is a real option for those who live the RV lifestyle. Yet another great way of earning an income to fund your travels. You are not just confined to using your cells or tablets either. Many camp grounds have internet access, sometimes for a small fee, but often for free. Many public areas now give free internet access, particularly cafes, bars and restaurants. So, there is a plethora of options to get online, and earn some money. You may be able to keep your current job by telecommuting, as it is often called. This is a popular and growing choice for many professionals. You can communicate with your employer by using applications (apps), such as Skype or Facetime. It is a great way to keep in touch with the boss, while you continue your travels.

Now that you have the option to work online, we will introduce some of the popular ways of earning money, simply by using your internet access.

ONLINE AUCTION SITES:

Online auction sites are a great way to earn extra cash, and can also be fun to run. The most popular one, eBay, has been going for over 20 years, and selling on there has never been simpler:

Register for an eBay account, at no cost whatsoever. Begin by creating private listings. Once you build up your stock, change to a business account with a store, at a later date.

Register for a Paypal account, also at no cost. Paypal runs like an online banking system, and enables you to receive payments or buy things yourself. Paypal is growing ever popular with many online shops, and is useful when you are traveling. It can link up with your personal bank account, making it simple to transfer money.

Quick and Easy - both of the above can be set up in a matter of minutes. Once you have an eBay and Paypal account, you can start selling to the recently estimated 160 million eBay members, worldwide. Don't just stick to selling to customers in your own country. Be confident and sell your wares overseas, all you need is access to a post office, or other courier such as FedEx.

The list of products you can sell on eBay are limitless, from RV's to VCR's. You could sell your artisan products, as we mentioned previously. If you are not craft minded, then there are still plenty of alternative options.

eBay often offer a number of free listings, so make the most of those. Other offers are and reductions in final value fees, that's the fee you pay when your item sells. If you have around 100 items for sale on eBay, then it is more economical to run an eBay store, for a monthly fee. This gives you a more professional front and encourages customers to buy from you.

If retail is your choice of employment, then don't just limit yourself to online selling. You will find craft fairs and markets at many places you visit. Make the most of these selling opportunities to increase you income.

If you don't want to buy new or make your own stock , then consider selling pre-owned goods, that are in excellent condition and hardly used. You can find such items at flea markets and garage sales. Visit thrift stores where you can find some great bargains, and then sell them on through your online account. You can even look for bargains as a buyer on eBay, and then sell that same item through your own eBay account, at a profit. Whatever you choose, the options are vast, and your only real limitation is the storage space available for your stock. Some RVs have a large area under the fixed bed. You could particularly consider the RV with a small garage space. These are ideal if you want to be a moving shop, with plenty of storage space.

FREELANCE WRITING:

Another boon industry that can be accredited to the proliferation of the internet. There are more and more smaller publishers and clients that are now looking for writers through online websites. A great way of finding work if you want to do a bit of freelance writing. You could find yourself writing blog articles and product descriptions. Along with the more specialist areas of business, such as business plans, CVs, educational papers. If you are creative, you could even write fictional novels and non fictional self help guides, such as jam making, soap making etc. The ability to research topics online means anyone can be an semi-expert in many subjects. You don't need to be able to make soap, only to write about making it. For this you can research your topic online. and write all that you learn in your own words, giving clear and precise instructions.

The use of electronic book readers is also becoming a popular way to read books. Added to that, self publishing is now an easy process at sites such as Amazon. This all makes being a published author, so very reachable. All you need are good English writing skills, the ability to research varying subjects on the internet, and a little creative flair. Remuneration can be a little low to start with. Over time, you can build up a portfolio and excellent reputation as a reliable freelance writer. Soon you may find yourself earning top dollars. Then you can find regular work from clients that you can pick and choose yourself. Plus, many of the online freelance sites pay money earned into your Paypal account, if you choose that option.

WRITE A BLOG:

If you are a master of the prose, then why not consider writing your own travel blog. You could do this while still doing other freelance writing. While it will not be an immediate money spinner, running a blog has the potential to bring in some great followers. The more popular the blog becomes, then the more hits it will receive. This means that you could then look at selling advertising space on your blog, bringing in revenue or sponsorship.

With the addition of cheap digital cameras, you could soon be publishing a blog about the places you have visited and travelled to. Adding stunning color pictures for your viewers. It might surprise you how many "would be" RVers are out there, who would love to do what you are doing. They could potentially become new followers of your blog, eagerly awaiting your next post to see where you travels take you.

If you are an avid reader, you could offer your paid services to do book reviews, and interview authors on your blog. By charging small fees for these services, as well as the advertising option we discussed, you have another means of income. All small ways of paying your way through your travels.

DROP SHIPPING:

There is one way to avoid the problems of storage space, while selling products online. It is to use a group of wholesale retailers who drop ship their goods, straight to your customers. So what exactly is drop shipping?

It means you are a middle person in the line of a sale. You advertise the goods, but you do not actually keep them in stock. When your customer buys from you, you then order from the drop shipping supplier. They will ship the order straight to your customers on your behalf. It is important to have a reliable supplier who has a constant supply of the goods they advertise to you. This can be one of the major pitfalls of being the middle person. If you sell a product, and they inform you it is not available, all your hard earned reputation as a trustworthy seller may soon disappear. Though, it can, and is, practiced by many retailers.

Ideally you should have an organized mind, plus that all important access to the internet. Do your homework and find reliable drop shipping suppliers, who won't let you down. You could even have more than one.

The positive side of being a drop shipping retailer, is that you do not need to have any financial outlay. You also set your own prices at whatever level you wish, so the profit margin is up to you. With time and experience, this can be a lucrative business whilst on the road, but you will have to work hard at it. It will not be successful overnight.

SECTION SUMMARY

We have tried to cover a few easy options of earning a living, if you want to work while you live on the road. Further advice to anyone looking to make some extra cash, is do not limit yourself to just one of the options, do a few of them all at once.

Most of our suggestions are do-able for everyone, particularly the online options. There are some exceptions to jobs with labor intensive tasks, such as crop picking, where a certain amount of fitness is required.

Any one can sell online. It does not need any special skills. Except perhaps the ability to spot a bargain. This can actually be quite good fun, especially if you start to attend the auction houses where you will find collectables. Researching your findings can be half the fun of selling collectables. It is quite exhilarating to know that you have purchased something of worth, and paid next to nothing for it.

Even freelance writing is easier than you think. All you need is a good sense of English, spelling, punctuation and grammar, and you will be fine. Practice makes perfect.

Don't limit your options just because you have never done anything like that before, or feel that your skill sets won't fit. Try it and see, what have you got to lose?

Finally, don't forget to keep a record of your ingoing and outgoing finances, for your annual tax return! Keeping a good record of everything you have earned and all your overheads of running the business, is essential. Also, ensure you have the correct tax status, such as for volunteer work, where you are only receiving perks such as site fees or hook up. If you do get paid work, check if you are classed as self employed, or if they are deducting tax from you.

It might be worth taking appropriate advice when it comes to filling in your tax return. More so, if you have done a bit of everything and your tax return is going to a complicated one. You may have to pay an accountant's fee, but a professional could save you money in the long run. They will have full knowledge of what you can, and cannot, claim as tax write-offs, which could save on large tax bills.

We told you earlier in this book that you can be a full time Rv'er, and still be a respectable person. One word of warning, all the above suggestions are hard work. Working for yourself means working long hours, and most of the time for little pay, but it will be worth it. Any job is worth the effort, if it helps to fund your RV lifestyle.

Chapter 4: Finances for a Nomadic Lifestyle

For some, the whole point of downsizing to live this kind of life, is to reduce financial stresses. Such worries have become a ubiquitous part of modern living. Living in an RV can be less of a strain on your finances.You can now make your money go so much further. Some choose a simpler lifestyle for this specific reason, they are in debt and see it as a way to reduce that burden. There's no shame to that. By living simpler, you can begin to pay off some of that debt, until one day you will be free of it. Now, the richness of your life is the road, and not in a never ending quest to own materialistic items. Sure, you can still have your TV, and you should definitely own a cell phone and a computer or tablet. These will prove essential items for your new lifestyle. The difference being, you will rid yourself of the yearning need to upgrade with every new model. The list of things you HAVE to spend money has grown shorter, with your new RV lifestyle. You will still need to pay for the essentials of life, such as food, gas and site fees. Maybe even the loan for your vehicle (home), it should still leave you with more money in the pot. This means you are now able to do the things you enjoy doing. Even if you have children, the need to buy them the newest toys or gadgets will reduce. Not least because of the limited space you now live in. Everything will be on a smaller basis, including your spending. We've discussed the possibility of still working for a living. Let us now look at how to manage your smaller budget, including banking, taxes and insurance.

Banking:

Banking can be a little tricky for those who have no permanent place of residence. This is especially so, if you need to open a new account. Most of you may already have bank accounts, so this may not be too much of a problem. Though, If you do have a bank account before you embark upon your venture, check with your bank that you can still use it if you do not have a fixed abode. Once you are nomadic, not having a fixed address can become problematic. This is something you need to look into well before you set off. We will still look at banking and other issues that may be problematic. What to do with your personal money to keep it safe? It is important not to have too much cash laying around in your RV. We'll take a look at these, and a few more concerns that you can expect along the way.

Online Banking: One of the great boons of the 21st century is the proliferation of the internet. Couple that with the growth of the Smart phone industry. This improved internet connectivity means that online banking for RVers is a real prospect. Because of this technological growth, it is simple to keep up with your finances and bank account. You can manage it all via your computer, smartphone or tablet.

Paying bills is easy too. Most of the time this will be possible to do online. With dedicated websites whereby you can set up payments for all, or most of your bills, you pay them all in one place. Online banking, checking balances, even transferring money, all done with just a few clicks of the mouse.

Use Debit and Credit cards more, so you are carrying only a small amount of cash with you, at any given time. Accepted at most outlets all over the US, you will find them useful. Depositing payments can be a little more tricky, especially if your bank doesn't have a branch close to where you are staying.

Some online banking apps, on your phone or tablet, let you photograph and email personal checks, and accept this as a deposit. Alternatively, you could of course use the more traditional way, by posting your check to the bank, which will take longer to clear. Even paying other people, or receiving payments, can be easy and straight forward. Many major banks offer the option to transfer funds electronically, to other accounts. It is a quick and easy method and usually incurs no transaction fees. There is also the option to use your Paypal account for paying people, goods and services, and also for receiving payments too.

For those who do not have a bank account, or feel they do not need one, then there are other options available:

Pre Paid Debit Card: These are becoming ever popular if you do not have, or do not want, a bank account. Useable at ATM's, and similar to a bank debit card. You can use them anywhere that accepts Visa or Master card, dependent on which one you chose. Pay into them at cash points such as MoneyGram and Western Union. There are a choice of cash points in popular stores such as Walmart, Kroger and other popular outlets. You can even have any salary you earn, paid into them. The money is usually available immediately.

These cards do come with an array of different packages, and with varying fees for different services, so shop around to get the best deal. Look for minimal monthly fees, free depositing and withdrawals, some even have free online services. Whichever you choose, make sure it is widely accepted. These cards are usually linked to banks, but are not classed as a bank accounts. Although, you can do many things that as you would with a normal bank account. Transfer money around accounts and onto one of these cards, or pay money in at many of the available cash point places, such as the Post Office. There is often a small fee to purchase the card.

Remember: Your card needs to be flexible, and accepted in as many places as possible.

Tax:

US citizens must be aware federal taxes.

We've mentioned this topic a few times already, but it's worthy of a mention in more detail. Particularly so if you are going to be self employed, with income from different clients. Filling in your Tax Return is complex enough. The more information you have collated throughout the tax year, then the better you can help yourself. One advantage it is possible to do your Tax Return online, which is helpful for those of on the move.

Choosing State of Domicile - If you are going to be a full time RVer, and no longer have a fixed abode, then you will need to register in a domicile. This is necessary for your tax returns, voting, driving license, vehicle registration and inspection, and other official documentation. At first, you could chose the state that you have recently lived in, until you adjust to your new lifestyle. Once you have settled into life on the road, then you could look at registering your domicile within a state that suits your needs the most. The 2 most popular states with RVers to register as their domicile, are Texas and South Dakota. Nevada and Wyoming are also popular choices. This is because of their advantageous tax systems. Although that should not be the only consideration when choosing a state for domicile. It is worth mentioning at this point, that you should consider joining Escapees RV Club, who's headquarters are in Texas. They can give lots of advice on making Texas your primary domicile base. The club also helps with vehicle registration and driver's license, but we'll cover those later. You don't have to limit your travels to Texas, but it is an excellent state for your official dealings. Whichever state you choose, it is a good idea to chose a domicile base whereby you can register all necessary information online. This way, you are not committed to returning to base too much.

Local Taxes - Be wary of states claiming you as a resident, just because you have stayed there a long time. Or because you have worked there. You need to choose a state that is best for your personal needs, and not end up being domicile somewhere by accident. When working in various states, you could end up owing them local state taxes.

Much the same can be said if you decide to work overseas. You will need to learn the local laws on their tax regulations. Find out whether you should be paying their taxes on your income, while you are there. Chances are you won't earn enough over the year, because of your transient residency. Be responsible while working in various states, or other countries. Find out about their tax requirements in advance.

Business Expenses - If your RV is your your work place, then there is no traveling involved. Therefore, you cannot claim for any mileage. To claim ANY business expenses on your RV, could end up costing. You may end up with your RV classified as a commercial vehicle. This can cause problems, such as needing a different driving license (CDL). If your RV is classed as a commercial vehicle, then it will be subject to the same regulations that go with a commercial vehicle and driver. You will have to pay business insurance, have weigh ins, and much more. Ask yourself if it's worth it. Consider the reasons that we have outlined, before you try and claim business expenses on your vehicle.

Loan Repayments - You may be able to write off the interest on any loan you have on your RV. The IRS considers RVs as a second home, for tax purposes. This means that you can claim tax credits for installing modifications, such as Solar Panels. To ensure you receive all the necessary credits, it is advisable to consult with a tax assessor.

Property Tax - You also need to be aware of any property tax, which is dependent on the state you have chosen for your domicile. If they do charge this to RVers, then it will be calculated on the value of your vehicle, and anything you are towing. The charge should only be at your domicile base, and not the states you are visiting, or even working at. There are many online resources to find out which states charge property tax on RV's.

Tax can be tricky at the best of times, more so for those living life on the road. We recommend that you seek professional advice with regards to your responsibilities of tax. A professional will know exactly what you can claim for. Good advice will pay for itself, many times over.

Insurance:

One of the criteria for determining insurance costs is risk, and that is dependent on your domicile base. The higher the risk of the area you chose, then the higher your premiums will be. You will need to consider many factors when choosing your domicile. For example, some will have higher health insurance than others, if you do not fall under a government or retirement cover. On the issue of health cover, you will also want a portable program. Before you chose your domicile, you need to look into each factor of medical, vehicle and personal policy covers of that state. You may get a good rate in one state for one of them, but a high rate for one of the others which could cancel out any gain. You really do need to do your homework before you make the decision of where you register for your permanent domicile.

Voting:

This is where having a permanent domicile is essential. Your legal domicile address is the state for registering to vote. If you don't want to return to your domicile state to do this, then register well in advance for an absentee ballot. You may not chose to vote in local elections, as you don't live there, but it's useful for the national vote. There are moves by some states, who are trying to restrict the right of RVers to vote. Careful consideration should by given when deciding your legal domicile, if you feel that this is an important aspect in your life.

Mail:

Again, we have touched on this briefly throughout this book. It is an important factor, so let's look at the various options available, in more detail.

Friends and Family

Having your mail posted (or redirected, if you still have a base where your mail is already delivered to), to an address of someone you know, such as friends or family. This is a cheaper option as there should be no real cost, other than when they post it on to you. At least you have someone you can trust handling your mail. They can also dispose of the ever increasing junk mail we all seem to get. At an appropriate time, you could arrange for them to send it on in bulk, to a local post office, or camp ground, if the camp ground don't mind.

Post Office

The Post office in the US (USPS), will hold mail for up to 30 days, free of charge. To get this service you must book 2 weeks prior to requiring it. You can also file a forwarding address of another Post Office, free of charge, again, allow 5 days notice before the service begins. For this to work, you would need to know where you are going ahead of time. This service is only available within the US.

Traveling Mail Box

Organized by a commercial mail receiving agency. The USPS Form 1583 produces a certificate for a company to open your own mail on your behalf. They offer scanning services so you are able to view letters on a computer, tablet or cell phone.

For a fee you can register for different levels. The fee is dependent on how many letters / parcels you expect to receive a month. You will be able to read the scanned PDF versions of your letters online. Or, you can have mail / packages forwarded to you by the same company. A scan of the unopened envelope will be available to view online. This way you ca decide if you want the company to open it, and scan it's contents. Or, you can ask them just to send the unopened envelope to your forwarding address. This way highly personal mail remains private.

These companies have addresses situated all over the US, so you can chose which one is best for you. Inform everyone to send your mail to that address. Here's an outline of the services they provide;

They do try to separate out the obvious junk mail, so you are only paying for what looks like the most important mail, but this is not fool proof.

They can even receive mail that needs signing for.

They will post mail on to you, whenever you request it, for an extra charge.

They hold your mail for up to 60 days, within your agreement. There is a daily charge if time goes beyond this.

They will shred mail if you do not wish to keep it.

Chapter 5: A-Z GUIDE - Comforts of Living in an RV

We have touched briefly on RV home comforts, in previous chapters. In this chapter though, we will look in more detail at what comforts you can expect in your RV. Also, which comforts you will have to forgo. It might surprise you how few you will miss. It's all part of the balancing act, in whether you feel the RV lifestyle is the one for you.

Air Conditioning

A must for most RVers, especially in the warmer climes it will be essential for keeping comfortable. Let's not forget that you are living in a large metal box. It can soon become stifling in the heat, and freezing in the cold. Many modern RV's come with air conditioning already fitted. If yours does not, then it is worth purchasing a unit. It will pay for itself in terms of comfort. If you decide to fit an air conditioning unit, it will depend on the size of your RV, on the best model of choice. A larger RV will need a more powerful air con unit. Let's have a brief look at what is available:-

Roof Mounted Air Con units. These have a lot of throughput. They are usually between 13.500 and 18000 BTU's (thermal units). Whilst these units can cool efficiently, at around 14-18 amps per hour, dependent on size, they do use a lot of power. This is fine when hooked up in a trailer park. They can be a heavy drain on your battery if you are not hooked up to the central electricity system.

Window Fit Air Con units. These are the next best option for cooling your RV. They are fit over a suitable window. Some modifications may be necessary to secure their fitting. The walls of an RV are not made to take such a weight. These type of units are usually in the range of around 5000-8500

BTU's. They draw approximately 6-10 amps when running, dependent on size.

Portable Air Con units. Whilst handy because they are mobile, they often need to be vented to the outside, and come with a window kit. These are the most economical for initial outlay and running costs, but the least effective.

Whichever type you chose that is best for you, always remember to maintain it with regular checks such as:-

Clearing vents to stop the dirt clogging up.
Straighten any bent condenser fins (metallic blades).
Add motor oil to any ports (though they're often concealed on modern units).
Check the belt if it's an older system.
Look for any drip marks, indicating a leaky system.
Change any filters.
Clean out any tubes you can easily access.
Empty any water collection pans, if it has one.

Regular maintenance should ensure it will run as an efficient and effective system, keeping you cool.

Beds

Everyone feels so much better after a good nights sleep. With sufficient sleep, you are more able to face the day better, feeling rested and refreshed. Recommendations are that an adult should sleep for around 8-9 hours a day. One of the best ways to ensure you have a good night's sleep, is to ensure your is a comfortable bed. Beds should be one of the prime considerations when you are choosing your RV. If you intend to live in it, or use it for many months at a time, then ideally, you need an RV that has a permanent bed. There is nothing more tiresome than having to make the bed up every night. If space allows, then you need a full size bed. If you have to compromise on size. then at least ensure the bed has a comfortable mattress. If the bed is the type made up from the seating cushions, add a thin strip of memory foam to place on top of the cushions, once it's made up. This helps to make the sleeping area more comfortable. Because of the limitations of storage, try and keep your bed linen to a minimum. 2-3 pairs of everything per bed, should be enough to ensure you have clean bedding all the time.

Boondocking

Some people love wild camping. Waking up surrounded by a beautiful vista, with not another person in sight, for miles around. The added bonus is, it's free. Others don't like the thought of camping up all alone, with little in the way of civilization, close by. There are a few sensible rules and guidelines to boondocking: keep safe using your common sense, respect your environment, DO NOT leave litter, and DO NOT empty your waste there. Your waste is not nice for the locals, or for wildlife. Keep boondocking respectable so locals do not have reason to complain. Boondocking, for many, is the ultimate in RV living, by camping in remote areas. Often it is with magnificent views in hard to reach places. Plus, of course, it does help if you are on a limited budget, not having any cost for a night's camping.

Cell phones

The proliferation of the modern smart cellular phone, and data connections, is a real boon to RVers. It now means that you can have access to the internet, in most places of the USA. With the ever increasing coverage of Long-Term Evolution (LTE), you also have super fast internet by your phone. It gives you the ability to check your emails. You can download apps such as Sat Nav. Look up the weather, or find out what entertainment is available in the area you're visiting. It can all through the use of your cell. You can even tether other devices, such as computers and tablets. This means that you can access the internet with them as well. You cell becomes your wi-fi hotspot. A hotspot is a wireless connection to the internet, so this means using your phone as the access point.

*Change cell phone plan?
wifi info

Beware though, some carriers charge extra for this. Usually there is a limited amount of data allowance. If you go over this, you will incur extra charges on your cell phone bill. Choose your carrier with care, DOUBLE checking how much data connection you have available, as you travel the USA. The best option is to purchase a phone that is not tied to any carrier. This means that the phone is unlocked, or sim free. Then you will need to purchase a number of prepaid sim cards. By doing this, you will still get a set amount of data, usually 4gb. Change the sim to the correct coverage for the area, as you move around. All cellular providers have Data sims, all provided with a variety of data allowances.

Cleaning duties

Housekeeping duties are fewer in an RV due to its size. One way of keeping snug, is to make sure your home is always clean and tidy. A few minutes of regular routine cleaning, daily, is usually enough to ensure your small space remains comfortable. Here are a few suggestions for making sure that your RV home stays spic and span.

Create a cleaning roster. Make a list of daily and weekly tasks, such as washing up, cooking, putting pots away, emptying the waste tanks etc. Try and distribute the jobs fairly, amongst the RV occupants. Nothing will cause more resentment than one person doing more tasks than another. This roster should extend to other duties, such as cooking, making beds, and all tasks that you consider chores. Make sure everyone gets at least one day off a week from any chores whatsoever. You will all feel much better by sharing the tasks, and staying clean. Be easy on yourself. REMEMBER, you are now living "the life."

Correct Equipment. Make sure you have the correct cleaning fluids and equipment for your RV. For example, you can put a fresh smelling liquids into the flush of the loo. You could use the specialist floor wipes for your small area of floor space. This will also ensure the floor doesn't get wet. Use disinfectant sprays for surfaces, making sure everywhere is germ free in such a confined space. A long handled brush for sweeping the floors, or even a small vacuum if you have full carpeting. There's no need to make cleaning tasks complicated. If anything, try to make them easy. Then, you can get them out of the way quickly, and get on with enjoying your day, knowing that at the end of it, your home is clean and tidy.

Along with your meal planner, good organization makes life so much easier. It means that you don't have to think about who's doing what and when. Plan and share the jobs out, and soon they will become an automatic part of the daily routine. Don't forget to clean the outside of your van as well, keeping your home shiny inside and out.

Clubs

✱ more research

Become a member of RV clubs, and you will have a never ending supply of new friends and advice. Plus, you will have the advantage of discounts that are available to members only. Here's some of the popular ones, at time of writing:

Good Sam Club (http://www.goodsamclub.com)

Discounts
10% on camping fees at over 2000 of their sites.
30% at their retail outlets.
Save on fuel at Pilot Flying J outlets.
Save on Good Sam's Roadside Assistance Plans
Save on subscriptions to best selling RV magazines.

Other Support
Online services such as free trip planning.
Online communications with all the club's advice and other members of over 1.6million.
Planned events.
Volunteer networks you can join.
Insurance & Finance deals.
Plus many more.

RV Golfclub (http://www.rvgolfclub.com)

Cost around $50 for a year's membership.

Discounts FREE overnight parking at over 400 of their beautiful sites. All with stunning scenery and walks, though it is dry parking, with no hook ups. You can also enjoy any amenities of their hotels, FREE, while you park there. They offer discounts on facilities at their clubs, such as golfing, restaurants, shops.

There are many more, all offering similar benefits, and all likeminded to RV living and vacationing. Some even offer jobs, or will offer advice on where to find work. Join in their organized events, and meet your fellow RVers who are also on the road, living the life.

Cooking

Those of you fortunate enough to have a large RV, will have a good size kitchen area. Cooking is much the same as in a bricks and mortar home. These type of kitchens usually come equipped with a full size oven, and most white domestic goods. For those with smaller gallery type kitchens, they will not be so well equipped. With that comes certain restrictions. Here's a few ideas that will help make cooking less of a chore.

One Pot Meals. One of the biggest aids to RV cooking has to be the one pot meal. Throw all the ingredients into one pot, to cook. Everyone has a favorite one pot meal, and you can collect them as you meet new RV friends and swap recipes. If you've never done one pot cooking before, then check out the web. There are lots of great tasty recipes on there, such as pasta bakes, stews, casseroles and soups. Get yourself a crock pot (slow cooker). Prepare all the ingredients early in the day, to throw them in the pot. By you evening meal time, it will ready to eat, and taste delicious. All with a minimum of effort.

Microwave cooker. Great for ready meals or TV dinners. Most supermarket outlets have a wide stock of ready prepared meals. Often they take only minutes to cook, in a microwave. There are so many choice in this type of meal, that you could eat food from different continents everyday. Most are nutritious and tasty, but do avoid any that have high salt and sugar levels.

Equipment. Try and manage with the minimum of cooking utensils, to save on storage space. Whether you go for plastic, which is lighter, or ceramic for your crockery, is a personal choice. It's true that a meal tastes much better from pottery than from plastic, but plastic is lighter to carry around. Just have one pan of each size, and wash the pots after each meal so they're readily available. Buy kitchen equipment that will sit inside of each other. Buy plastic storage boxes with lids, to store the heavier equipment inside. You don't heavy things up in the higher cupboards. Always keep heavier stuff at floor level.

Plan Ahead, Be Healthy. The trick to successful RV cooking is to plan ahead. Try and make a menu with plenty of balanced meals, such as one day pasta, another day rice, salad and casseroles. A comprehensive list of meals will give you an idea of the ingredients needed. This will make your shopping chore easier. When you go shopping, take 3 meals from your menu list, and buy all the ingredients needed for those meals. Shopping this way means you spend less time in the store struggling to think up meals, leaving you more time for leisure activities. Try and keep a varied and mixed diet with plenty of fresh food. There is no excuse for unhealthy eating. Make eating out a treat, rather than a regular occurrence, as it can become expensive. An occasional treat now and then is good, but you are not a tourist on holiday, this is your way of life. Now you have time on your hands, read up about nutrition. Then you can provide you and your loved ones with healthy meals.

Dining out

Of course you do not have to cook all the time. You will be visiting some great places, so it's only natural that you will want to try out the local cuisine. It would be foolish not to take advantage of it. It's important to enjoy your newfound freedom, and have a few odd luxuries, such as the occasional dining out. To make your money go further, look for special offers and discounts. Restaurants often have a cheaper rate at quieter times of day, sometimes known as, "early bird?" Some national chains have discount cards. When you eat in one of their restaurants, you build up points. When the points have built up, you redeem them on your bill. Let's not forget the pensioners' specials, if you are retired. Be astute, and search for the offers. Then eating out will not break the bank.

Downsizing

This is worth a mention as it is probably one of the hardest tasks you will do, when in comes to moving to an RV lifestyle. Restricted space means that you will not be able to take all your possessions with you, and why would you want to? This is a new way of living. A more uncluttered and less regimented lifestyle. Downsizing does not have to be painful. You can even make money, by selling your excess belongings. Use the extra cash to fund your life on the road. Go the whole way, and sell your home outright, so you can fund your new found freedom. It is liberating and cathartic, once you've rid yourself of the many hoarded possessions. You will never want to return to your old way of life. Few do. If you can't bring yourself to sell the family home, then think of renting it out. It will provide a useful income while you travel, and it doesn't have to be an extra burden. Hire a letting agent to do all the hard work. REMEMBER, you are un-cluttering your life of possessions and responsibilities.

Energy

Despite having downsized and forsaken many consumer goods, you will still need some level of comfort in the form of modern appliances. Watching TV, listening to music, having a cooler, toaster, cooker etc. All of which will need run off electricity or gas. You could consider manufacturing your own electricity, by using a generator, and, or, solar panels.

The simplest generators have been around for years. Powered by a fuel such as gasoline or diesel, though some use propane. The concept is simple; an engine drives an alternator. In turn, this generates a 110v AC electricity, for you to use in your RV. Traditional generators can be quite bulky and noisy, although there are silenced models available. More recently, inverter generators in production. These are much smaller and lighter, as they only provide power as and when you use it. This makes them more economical to run.

Another power option is solar panels. These work better in sunnier states, and can provide a useful amount of electricity, especially for the boondockers. There are some limitations to using solar panels, such as they do not provide as much power as a generator. If you are camping in a remote area, they can provide the electricity you need to keep functioning for a few days.

Equally, always have a spare gas bottle for when you have to switch over to using the gas supply. You should also carry a second, charged leisure battery. This is ideal if you are in a situation where you are unable to connect to a power supply to charge your leisure battery.

Heating

Not all your traveling will be in the warmer climes, especially if you're a full timer. Winters can be cold in some areas of the

US. Even if you travel in search of the sun, you will still have times when you need some heating to keep the cold at bay.

Air Con. Those who have a good Air Con unit may, have one that also provides blown heat. These types usually have a heating element inside, and will blow warm air into your RV when you need it.

Sealing. There are a few other ways of keeping your RV cosy, when the temperature drops. Much will depend on the system in your vehicle. All RV's will have some form of heating, but older models are not very efficient. Coupled with a van that may not be well insulated. A good way to avoid letting in the cold, is to seal up any drafts, such as around the doors and windows. As they age, the rubber seals can crack and allow air in. If you keep them well maintained, then they will last a long time. Once the sealants have cracked, they will need replacing. You also need to check your outside seals, this is a way for ingress of both water and draft. Using sealant can sometimes help to solve this, even if it's only temporary.

Heating All this work will be pointless, if your furnace is not working to its maximum efficiency. Keep it well maintained, and have it serviced regularly, especially if it runs from gas. Not only to keep yourselves toasty warm, but also to keep you safe. You can supplement your furnace, by purchasing secondary heating. This means having space heaters, or an electric oil radiators. Should you decide to use electric heaters, then choose a system that isn't noisy. Fan heaters can keep you warm, but also keep you awake all night.

Maps

We keep extolling the benefits of internet access. The use of Sat Nav's can be great, but, we cannot stress the benefits of using manual maps, enough. Call it an old fashioned concept, but you cannot beat looking at a physical map. Wherever possible get a map of where you are visiting. If nothing else, it will help you to plan your trip well in advance. If you know where you are going, then you can look up on the internet to do research on the area. find out the advantages and disadvantages of certain towns, cities and states. A map though, especially if you have a driving partner, is the best way to find your way around. When you are in a city, it's worth purchasing a map of the city streets. This will save your poor feet as you should not get lost and walk around in endless circles. Mind you, getting lost can be a part of the adventure too, but only if you have plenty of time and energy. Keep those maps together in a file, so if you return back to that area, you won't need to buy another. You'll soon find you have a great collection of maps, all proving useful at some time or other.

Roads

Something that you will have an abundance of. The key to your freedom.

Tolls. Try to avoid roads with tolls, particularly if you are visiting overseas. There are always other routes, especially if you are not in a rush.

One Way. Be extra vigilant of one way roads. There is nothing worse than being stuck on a one way road with a huge vehicle, and all the locals are waving frantically at you as you attempt to turn around. Same goes for narrow streets, look out for the max width and height signs.

Road Signs. Ensure you know and fully understand these in every country you are driving in. Particularly if you go to certain countries in Europe, such as the UK, where everyone drives on the other side. This will feel weird on a roundabout, but you must, must, understand what is expected of you. After all, you don't want any dents in your lovely home.

Services. Learn to say no to buying lunch every time you stop at the road lay-by service stations. You have the means to make your lunch and a decent cup of coffee, use it. Otherwise it can soon get expensive.

Chapter 6: Safety Whilst Living a Full-time RVer

If you followed our advice, then you're just about ready to begin the adventure of a lifetime. So far our book has:

Helped you choose an RV, that is specific to your needs.
Advised you on how to keep cool in the summer, and warm in the winter.
Guided you on the essential equipment.

Now, it's time to look at one of the most important elements of your adventure: Safety.

This encompasses many factors including:

Road safety.
Personal safety.
Security of your possessions.

You are going to spend your life on the road. No matter how good a driver you are, you can still come across accidents. In fact, the longer you drive, the greater the chance of it happening to you. Our advice here may help to reduce that risk. Your RV is an expensive item, and as such could make you a target for crime. A few simple steps can keep your RV safe.

Finally, there's the problem of your personal possessions. Whilst your RV will not be as secure as a traditional home, you can take certain measures to keep your possessions safe and secure.

DRIVING

First, and most important, the aspects of safety that should concern you, will be the safe handling of your RV, and mastering it on the road. For many people this will be by far the biggest vehicle they have ever driven. Give yourself time to get used to its large size, and remember, it DOES NOT drive the same as a Dodge Pick-up. It takes far longer to come to a stop. Cornering is a whole new skill set, and reversing needs a completely different approach than a car. With practice, and careful road handling, it will soon become second nature and you'll soon be driving like a professional.

When driving on the freeway, it can seem that your RV is even easier to handle than a standard car. As you sit in your high seat, up off the road, with power steering to ease the flow, you will feel safe. DO NOT be fooled. There could still be problems ahead, especially when you leave the freeways and head into town.

* *City Driving and Cornering* - RV's need a wider turning radius, to ensure the vehicle has cleared the curb. Often the front wheels are actually behind the driver, so you need to advance further into the road, before turning. This in itself can cause problems, as you will move nearer the other side of the road, if not actually move into it. You need to ensure there is no oncoming traffic before you move over. If all is clear, make sure you have room to make the turn, for example no parked vehicles blocking your manouver.

* *Signalling* - This needs to be clear, and done well in advance, but not too soon to confuse other road users. Insure there are no possible misunderstandings, and other

drivers understand your intentions. REMEMBER, if you are turning right, then you will need to swing out to the other side of the road. How far is dependant on the size of your RV. This may confuse other drivers, so watch out for any that have moved between you and the curb, or have even tried to overtake you.

* *Turning* - Take it steady as you turn. Take your time, keeping a keen eye on your wing mirror to insure you have left enough space. If you are in any doubt, then STOP. If all is clear, then don't be afraid of trying to reverse back, to attempt the corner again. It may well cause problems in waiting traffic. That is a better option than a huge insurance bill, because you've rushed the turn. This could lead to your own vehicle getting damaged, and maybe another. Even worse, someone getting hurt.

* *Be Aware* - Learn to judge the width and height of your own vehicle. Height is the obvious one. Always be aware of low over passes, or height barriers across parking lots. Width is often the least considered aspect of your RV's size, but is just as important. If you are unfamiliar with an area, and find yourself entering a small narrow road, park up. Get out of your vehicle and check it out on foot. Or, send a passenger to check it out. It might seem like over kill, but it beats having to reverse back down a narrow street, because you cannot drive any further.

* *Braking* - One of the most important safety aspects you need to be aware of, and take into consideration when you are driving. There is a huge difference in braking distance between an RV, and a standard car, or smaller van. The huge size and weight of an RV, means it will keep on going. It will continue well after the point that a standard vehicle

would have stopped, once the brakes are applied. You must be aware of this when braking, and allow enough time and distance to stop in a safe manner. If you are towing with your RV, then you must be aware of brake fade. This can happen when brakes become overheated, because of heavy use. To help combat this issue, try and use lower the gears as often as is possible, to slow the vehicle down. This is especially so if driving downhill.

* *Climbing and Ascending inclines.* - Your vehicle is far heavier than a standard car. There are obvious factors you need to consider, when you are climbing or descending a steep hill. Understand your RV and where the ideal power band is for your vehicle, when climbing hills. This is the engines capacity to produce the most horsepower for climbing hills. Usually this will be one of the lower gears. Familiarize yourself with the gear that the RV is most comfortable with, and drive steadily up the hill. If you try and push your engine too hard in the wrong gear, it may overheat. Chances are you will be moving slower than other vehicles on the incline, but still be aware of them. Should you create a tailback of over five cars, than try to find a suitable place where you can pull over and allow them to pass. They will be grateful to you, and you should get lots of smiles and waves, making it worth your while.

Going down hill also has its problems, along with unique solutions. When descending a steep incline, make sure you are in a low enough gear to control the speed of the RV. It is best if you try not to use the brakes too much. This will put full strain on them. Brakes are for stopping, not for slowing down, so use them if you need to stop. As mentioned in the previous section on braking, overheating brakes can cause brake fade. This will severely reduce the efficiency of them, which on a steep hill could be disastrous. Just let the engine take the strain, whenever it is safe to do so on the decline. Giving it only "occasional" assistance with the brakes. Like all driving in your RV, "slow and easy," is the watch phrase.

* *Manoeuvring* - We stress once again, REMEMBER that you are driving a large vehicle. You cannot drive as though it is your family mini-van. Driving traits, such as speeding, tailgating, weaving in and out of traffic, are NOT recommended. Sudden changes of lanes, especially at speed, can cause the RV to become unstable. It is a huge powerful vehicle, and will take all your concentration to handle safely. Drive steady, stick to your lane whenever possible. If you do move out to overtake, then do not leave it till the last minute. Leave plenty of distance between you and the vehicle in front. Follow basic common sense, and you should reach your destination in one piece.

* *Reversing or Parking* - For many, this is often one of the first problems they may encounter, when they first start to drive their RV. There is no need to be overwhelmed by it. Like most of the practical stuff here, the more you do it, the better your will get. Here are a few pointers to help you become an expert at reversing, and parking your RV:

* Do you have **reversing cameras?** If so, utilize them. They are not essential, but they are helpful. You will find them useful in judging how close you are to any obstacles behind you. Or, how close you are to any walls at either side of you.

* **Assess the space** you are attempting to park in. Get out of the driving seat, and judge it beforehand. If you are uncertain that your RV will fit, then move on to somewhere else. Better to do that than risk damaging yours and other

peoples' vehicles. Parking spots for a vehicle this size can be few and far between. Don't let that cloud your judgement when it comes to parking. Remember the mantra, if it doesn't look like it will fit, then it won't.

* Make sure that you have **good all round visibility**. Don't just concentrate on the rear, you need to check the sides too. Open all your curtains so none of the windows are not covered. Make full use of those side mirrors.
* If you have a **passenger**, use them. They can watch for you as you line up to park. DO NOT rely solely on their judgement. DO NOT blame them if all goes wrong.

* *High Winds* - A nightmare for all RV owners. The height of the vehicle makes them susceptible to rolling over, especially if the wind is side on. Should you find yourself in such a situation, here's a few pointers to help reduce the risk:

* **Slow down.** This will help you maintain control of your RV, should you a strong gust of wind hit you. Remember to keep to the minimum speed limit, and try not to impede other drivers. DO NOT oversteer to compensate for the wind. This can increase the instability.
* If you feel completely uncomfortable, or feel the situation is too dangerous to continue, **don't be afraid to stop** at the first opportunity. Find a suitable and safe place. Try and find shelter for your RV, such as an underpass, to offer protection. If this is not possible, then park it so that your vehicle is facing head on into the wind. Once you have found somewhere suitable, then sit it out and wait for the winds to subside, before continuing your journey. You are an RVer now, it is not necessary to hurry to your destination. Sit down, relax, make a cup of coffee.

These are just some of the situations that you may find different to the usual vehicle you drive. There is no need to be daunted. Practice makes perfect. If it helps set your mind at ease, there are a number of RV training courses that you can enrol in. These can vary between basic driving, as we have tried to outline here. Or a full intensive course that will teach you similar skills to those who are learning to drive a truck. You will find these type of courses especially useful in learning how to park and reverse your RV.

Following, are a few further pointers, which may seem glaringly obvious, but are easy to overlook:

Stop For Regular Rests:

It is important for you and your family, that you don't drive while tired. It is easy to tire while driving such a large vehicle, especially on a hot day. Stop for rests. Allow yourself a certain mileage everyday, or a certain amount of time for driving. You don't have to stick to it, especially if you tire earlier than you planned. Don't go beyond your targets either. Remember, you're an RVer now, there's no need to rush anywhere. Stop regular and stretch those limbs, ease any stiff muscles, visit the toilet, eat and drink. It will also help you unwind from the intense concentration of driving. If there is more than one driver among your group, all the better. This will allow you to rotate driving, while the other rests.

Never stop in the breakdown or emergency lane to swap drivers. It is for emergencies only, respect that. There will be plenty of picnic areas to pull over, or service areas.

Bad Weather Plans:

It is important that you have a strategy for severe weather conditions. You don't want to be traveling in heavy rain or high winds, as we've already discussed. If possible, stay where you are, until it clears. Research the local climate of where you are traveling to. Check the local weather forecast before you travel. Be aware of the likelihood of storms and high winds, especially if you are in tornado country. If you decide to have some vacation time in a mountainous region, such as a ski ing holiday, find out where the storm shelters are. Keep yourself safe, so others don't have to risk their lives saving you, because you did not take precautions and use common sense. Oh, and have a few board games at the ready, incase your rained in. This is where the gas bottles and extra leisure battery can be handy. Should you have to pull over while the bad weather eases.

Maintenance:

Keep your vehicle well maintained. Yes, it can be expensive, but it will pay for itself in the long run. Try to learn a few of the unskilled mechanical jobs yourself. Regular checking of the oil levels, filters, tire pressure, water and seals are all simple jobs you can learn to do yourself. If you're hiring an RV, check who's responsible for what, in regards to the vehicle's maintenance. Good Breakdown recovery is essential too. Towing will be expensive, if you don't have full breakdown coverage. Think ahead, and take out an all round recover service deal. Also, renew any extended warranties that are due. This will cover many mechanical failures.

Emergency Kit:

Always have certain items at hand: first aid box, maps, full water bottles, and even food rations. Have enough of these items to see you through a few days, incase you are unable to restock your provisions.

PERSONAL SAFETY

It would be ironic if you have thrown off the shackles of living the rat race, just to be encumbered by a new fear of crime. In all likelihood, if you follow a few simple precautions, you will be as safe in your RV, as you were in your brick home. These following suggestions will help you to reduce the chances of being a victim of crime.

* *Free Camping* - For many, the freedom of the road, and being able to camp up wherever is possible, is one of the main attractions to RV living. Wild camping, or Boondocking, has many followers. For most people, they manage it in complete safety. Boondocking is often in remote areas, such as wild forests, or even the deserts. This can actually work to your advantage, as there are fewer people around, and therefore less opportunity for thieves. It is still useful to take precautions. If you feel uncomfortable in an area, then move on. Life is too short to be laying awake at night worrying. Join a Boondocking club, which will have a list of safe boondocking sites. If you're a pet lover, then you could always take your dog with you. The barking will alert you to any prowlers around your RV, and also act as a deterrent so they should scarper.

* There are a number of other free options for wild camping - truck stops, parking lots of major store chains such as Walmart and Kmart. Restaurant chains such as Cracker

Barrel, and even fast food joints such as McDonalds. Although many of these places are happy for RVers to spend the night, it is always best, and courteous, to speak to the manager first. With regards to your safety in these free pull up grounds, once again common sense should prevail. Do not park in an area you are uncomfortable with. Choose a spot you are happy to walk around at night, maybe a well lit spot. If the area is unfamiliar, then a quick google search to see if you can find the recorded crime statistics for the area, may put you at ease. As we have already stressed, if you're uncomfortable, then move on.

* *Camping Grounds* - This is where most RVers stay, especially the novice. Most sites are well regulated and often well lit. Having property stolen from a well managed site is rare, even if you have left items out overnight. If staying on one of these sites, you can still try and park in a well lit area. Make sure you have the relevant phone numbers of the security firm, if they have any. If not, then get the Site Manager's number. No matter where you camp or park, always remember to lock your RV when you leave, including doors, windows and roof vents. The experience of burglary, or even worse, having your RV stolen, will not be a good one. Practice preventative measures, which we will now have a quick look at.

The final section in our safety guide, will concentrate on keeping your personal valuables safe and secure.

LOCKING UP YOUR VEHICLE

This seems to be stating the obvious, yet it is all too easy to forget to lock your vehicle when you go out. Needless to say, lock the doors and windows when you are going anywhere. Lock and cover the safe, if you have one. If you do have a safe, try to make sure it is well hidden. It might also help if you have a locking device on your RV, such as a clamp on a wheel. If towing an RV, consider a kingpin lock, which stops unauthorized decoupling. That way your towing vehicle should be safe as well, if it's still hitched together. Pull down the blinds so any would be intruders don't know if anyone is in or not. This may advertise you are out, during the day, but it's better that outsiders cannot see in. An added bonus of shutting blinds or curtains is that it will keep the sun out, also helping to keep your RV cool. Lock any small lockers that placed on the outside, particularly if the locker is situated under a bed, on the inside. This is easy access to the inside of your RV home.

Locks - Increase the security of your RV by improving the entry locks, and any locks on the external lockers. Often the locks on the doors of RVs are not as secure as they should be. Replacing it, or adding another, will help protect your RV home. If it does not already have them, then fit dead bolt locks that are more secure than the standard latch door lock. Also, the external compartment locks are often a standard key, identical to many other RV's. In theory, this means that anyone with a similar RV can open your locks.

Alarms, Trackers and Lighting - Some high end RVs already have such extra security already fitted. If yours has not, then you could consider fitting such items, to improve security. These can vary from a simple system that sounds an alarm, should someone attempt to break into your RV. Or one that will track and report the RV location, if your vehicle is stolen. External motion detector lights can be a good deterrent too. Thieves prefer the dark as it increases their anonymity. If you have not got external lights then consider parking in a well lit area.

Finally, just remember the obvious - do not leave valuable items in plain sight. Keep them locked away in a safe, or at least in a hidden place. If you are away at night, consider leaving the lights on. If anything, this will leave the thieves guessing whether there is anyone home.

BE PREPARED - If the worse comes to the worse, then make sure that you are ready to deal with the consequences. Keep a list of all your valuables. You could even take photographs of them, particularly if there is a unique mark that will identify the item as yours. If necessary, have your property valued by an appraisal professional, and marked. Photograph high value items, and keep those photos and your valuations away from your RV. Keep such documents at your main home if you have one, or in a safety deposit box, or with a relative or friend. Don't forget those all important insurance documents at hand, for loss or damage. That way, should you have the misfortune of being a victim of a crime, then you will have the funds to carry on, regardless.

Fear of crime is often said to be far higher than the actual incidence of crime. Victims can become totally debilitated by the effects. It is not our intention in this book, to alarm anyone. Reports of RVers being subject to any crimes are actually quite rare. Even for those who boondock and free camp in parking lots. That is not to say that you should not take sensible precautions. Some of the suggestions we have given you, may help reduce the small chance that your family might fall victim to crime.

Summary

You have reached the end of your journey in this book.

It is hoped that you have come to the decision, that the simple RV life is the future for you. Perhaps you are are already on the road, and looking for more ideas, by reading how others are living the nomadic lifestyle. Whatever your personal situation, we hope you have found some useful information between these pages. The information you have gleaned from this book, will set you in good stead for your life in your RV. Making you better prepared to face many of the situations that could arise. Of course, we have not been able to cover everything, but we should have helped to make your journey a more positive experience.

For those who do choose the RV lifestyle, then usually the main reason for doing so, is the freedom. It is important to remember this when you are on the road. It can become all too easy and tempting, to end up staying longer in one place longer than you intended, and setting down roots. While that in itself is not a bad thing, to some degree it defeats the main goal, of living in an RV. Don't become too static at any time, because there is always so much to see and do.

We have mentioned many times in this book, the advantages of RV living. Those Positives may be a different experience for everyone. Freedom though, is something that appeals too many RVers. When it actually comes down to it, and they are living the RV lifestyle, it can turn out to be the complete opposite of what they expected. Do not be surprised if that happens to you. Often, living in such close proximity to another person, even someone who you love and cherish, can put a strain on the most stable of relationships. If you find this is happening to you and your loved ones, or if the lifestyle is not what you had hoped it would be, then maybe it is time to think about an alternative. If you have committed everything to your RV dreams, and it turns into a nightmare, then it can be difficult to return to your former lifestyle. It is possible, but may be slow. This is where a trial run can be useful. If you can hire an RV van for an extended period to try it out, then all the better. If finances allow, buy your vehicle before selling your home. Perhaps renting your home short term, while you try out the lifestyle. At least then you will have some idea of whether you are suited to living in an RV full-time. If the lifestyle does not feel right, for whatever reason, then yat least you can return back to your former home. Just sell the RV on, or keep it for future holidays on the road. Sure, you will lose some capital, but you will have learned about a whole new way of living. You can mark it up as an experience to your lifelong adventures, and tick it off as tried and tested.

Though, it is not just the smaller living space that you will need to adjust to, in your new life. As we have mentioned in this book, you need to prepare for a complete change of many of the things you take for granted. Every aspect of your life is going to be different. From the simplest of things, such shopping for groceries, to the more complex details, such as managing your finances. Even socializing will be a whole different experience. It is unlikely that many of the new people you meet, will be around for long. Most of them will be passing acquaintances. Every destination is likely to provide a whole new set of people. Though, if you continue in this lifestyle long enough, you will start to see the same faces popping up every now and again. For some, this is the essence of living this kind of life, meeting different people all the time. For others, they may prefer the familiarity of old and trusted friends. Of course, if you plan and organize everything well, then there is always the option of arranging to meet with familiar faces en route. Pop in to visit family. Arrange a mutual destination with other travellers, so you can all meet up. It means you you still get to spend time with those who make you happy.

We have tried to cover most aspects of RV living. How to buy the right RV and then equip it to your personal requirements.

How to earn a living. How to keep safe on the road, and how to maintain and clean your RV. Such things may seem obvious, you already do much of it in a traditional home anyway. You might be surprised at the differences, once you downsize to a smaller and more mobile space. It is not overstating the fact that EVERYTHING in your life will need to downsize, and you will soon become a minimalist. Even down to your wardrobe. If you are a hoarder, then this will be a good time to overcome old habits. There is no room for putting things that you don't need aside. In this book, we have already touched on the subject of downsizing. It can be a daunting task, because you will have to part with many memories. The memories will never leave you though, they will always be a part of who you are. You could photograph the items that you are disposing of, then you still have a picture to remember them by.

Sometimes it seems that the world is getting smaller, with such quick means of travel in today's technical era. You should extend your travels outside of the USA. Perhaps as a novice RVer it is advisable to stay in your own country to start with. Once you become a seasoned traveller, then the whole world is available to you. Not just across the border to Mexico either. Shipping your RV to Europe is an option. Although it can be expensive, many prefer having their own RV, in preference to hiring one. You need to be aware though, that some European roads and camp sites are on a smaller scale than the US. They may not be able to accommodate the largest Class A RV. Although you will see these types of vehicle on the road, they are not as popular as they are in the US. Another consideration is the difference in voltage. In many European countries, electricity is 220-240v rather than 110v. This means that you will need a voltage converter, so you don't damage your electrical goods. Further, European RVers tend to buy their gas by the bottle, and just replace an empty one with a full one. Although, there are an increasing number of places to fill your propane tanks. If you do decide to travel abroad, remember to write and record everything you experience along the way. Then you have a log of a treasured memory, for later in life. This would be an excellent opportunity to produce that travel blog. Tell the world about your adventure.

FREEDOM has always played an important role in the history of humankind. It is a part of our progress and our psyche, to have freedom of choice in the decisions we make in our lives. Many of us are raised to be educated for a career. Then we will work until we retire. We do this because it is the accepted way, to work and consume. To earn money to join the world of consumerism. It is hard to break the mold of this expected pattern of life. It is a brave choice to leave the protection of the "norm." Yet, that is what a nomadic life is all about. Yes, you will still work for a living. Yes, you will still enjoy a few modern comforts in life. But, no, you do not have to work 9-5, and nor do you have to stay in one place to do so. Living the RV lifestyle usually means you are your own boss. For the most part, you can live life off the grid, if that is what you yearn to do.

Finally, we would like to thank you for purchasing and reading this book. Much of the contents and thoughts are written from experience. We truly hope it will be of some help to you in your own future travels. Most full time RVers are retired, but there are families who partake in this lifestyle, and others who simply chose to opt out of the accepted way of life, so young or old, age is no limitation. And, who can blame them. Of course, if do have children then there are other aspects, such as home schooling, but that would be another story for another book.

Stay Safe and Stay mobile.

Good Luck and Bon Voyage.

Made in the USA
Middletown, DE
22 July 2018